AIR CAMPAIGN

EASTERN FRONT 1945

Triumph of the Soviet Air Force

WILLIAM E. HIESTAND | ILLUSTRATED BY JIM LAURIER

OSPREY PUBLISHING
Bloomsbury Publishing Plc
Kemp House, Chawley Park, Cumnor Hill, Oxford OX2 9PH, UK
29 Earlsfort Terrace, Dublin 2, Ireland
1385 Broadway, 5th Floor, New York, NY 10018, USA
E-mail: info@ospreypublishing.com
www.ospreypublishing.com

OSPREY is a trademark of Osprey Publishing Ltd

First published in Great Britain in 2024

A catalog record for this book is available from the British Library.

ISBN: PB 9781472857828; eBook 9781472857835; ePDF 9781472857842; XML 9781472857811

24 25 26 27 28 10 9 8 7 6 5 4 3 2 1

Maps by www.bounford.com
Diagrams by Adam Tooby
3D BEVs by Paul Kime
Index by Fionbar Lyons
Typeset by PDQ Digital Media Solutions, Bungay, UK
Printed and bound in India by Replika Press Private Ltd.

Title page: Red victory: a formation of Soviet Il-2M Shturmovik ground-attack aircraft in flight over the ruins of Berlin, 1945. (From the fonds of the RGAKFD in Krasnogorsk via www.Stavka.photos)

Glossary

German terms:

Fliegerkorps: Air Corps
Geschwader: Air Wing
Gruppe: Air Group
JG (*Jagdgeschwader*): Fighter Wing
KG (*Kampfgeschwader*): Bomber Wing
Kriegsmarine: German Navy
LG (*Lehrgeschwader*): Operational Training Wing
Luftflotte: Air Fleet
SG (*Schlachgeschwader*): Ground Attack Wing

Soviet terms:

ADD: *Aviatsiya dal'nego deystviya*
Front: Soviet formation equivalent to Western army group
GVF: Civil Air Fleet
PVO (*Voyska protivovozdushnoy oborony*): Forces of Air Defense
Stavka: Soviet supreme high command
VA (*Vozdushnaya Armii*): Air Army
VVS (*Voyenno-vozdushnye sily*): Soviet Air Force
VVS-VMF (*Voyenno-Vozdushnye Sili Voyenno-Morskoy Flot*): Naval Air Force

CONTENTS

INTRODUCTION

An Il-2M2 Shturmovik ready for a mission. The most produced and famous Soviet aircraft of the war, the heavily armored Il-2M2 provided powerful support to the series of Red Army offensives that drove the Wehrmacht to the Vistula in late 1944. (Courtesy of the Central Museum of the Armed Forces, Moscow via www.Stavka.photos)

The Red Army launched a series of massive offensives across Poland and East Prussia in 1945, and after five months of brutal fighting ultimately fought its way into the ruins of Berlin. The Soviet military machine that won these victories had become a true combined arms force, using firepower and mechanization to smash through Axis defenses and launch deep exploitation operations that rivaled those of the early-war Wehrmacht. The Soviet Air Force, the *Voyenno-vozdushnye sily* (VVS), was a key component of this war machine. The VVS had suffered crippling losses in the early months of the war but had battled the Luftwaffe to a standstill in 1942 and 1943. Improved aircraft and aircrew allowed Soviet airmen to play a vital role supporting the 1944 offensives that destroyed entire German army groups and drove the Wehrmacht from the USSR and the Balkans. In January 1945, the air armies of the VVS were poised on the Vistula River with the Red Army's powerful fronts, ready for the final assault into Germany.

The Luftwaffe, crippled by years of grinding attrition and forced to spread its dwindling squadrons between multiple fronts, could only hope that its small but potent force of jet fighters and other new technology weapons would stem the tide. Although German jet operations against the USAAF and RAF receive much attention in postwar accounts of the Luftwaffe's last months, the vast majority of its sorties in 1945 would actually be flown on the Eastern Front as aircraft and scarce fuel were shifted to face the final Soviet offensives. German pilots, many still flying outdated Bf 109s and Ju 87s, would even briefly claw back air superiority from the VVS in February before fighting to the end over Berlin.

This volume describes the final clashes of Soviet and German airmen as Zhukov's, Konev's, and Rokossovsky's fronts battled to the Oder in January 1945, cleared their northern and southern flanks in February and March, and launched the final assault on Berlin in April. The Red Army offensives of 1945 shaped the history of the second half of the 20th century, securing Soviet dominance over Eastern Europe and sealing the division of the continent into communist and free world alliances. Soon after the war, the USSR would begin to equip its units with new jet fighters, long-range bombers, and nuclear weapons, and a decade later the Luftwaffe would be reborn as part of a new anti-communist Western alliance. The Soviet doctrine for the aviation operations that won the Battle for Berlin, now paired with nuclear weapons, would threaten NATO forces for decades to come.

Soviet aircraft over a tank column in 1943. By 1945, even the USSR was running short of troops to hurl unsupported at German machine guns, and the Soviet army relied heavily on firepower in the form of artillery, air support, and tanks to improve its combat power and limit infantry casualties.(Print Collector via Getty Images)

ORIGINS

In the spring of 1944, Hitler's Germany could still nurse hopes of averting ultimate defeat. The Wehrmacht held Western Europe, much of Italy, and the Baltic States and Belorussia in the USSR. In France, Hitler massed his ground forces in hopes of repelling the expected Allied invasion across the Channel. The Luftwaffe fielded 4,500 combat aircraft – roughly the number in the force at the start of Operation *Barbarossa* in 1941 – and hoped that the revolutionary Me 262 jet fighter and other new weapons in development would allow it to regain its former competitive edge. Under pressure to ward off the Allied bombing offensive, the Luftwaffe starved the Eastern Front of aircraft, planning to surge aircraft to prepared airfields in France when the Allies landed.

Instead, 1944 brought a series of disastrous defeats that dashed German hopes. USAAF strategic bombers began a renewed daylight assault on the Reich in the spring, this time with its bombers escorted by long-range P-51 Mustang and P-47 Thunderbolt fighters that inflicted heavy attrition on the German fighter force. The Allied invasion of France in 1944 rapidly overwhelmed what opposition the Luftwaffe could offer, and the subsequent Allied breakout and drive to the German border overran much of its air defense radar network. In the East, the Red Army destroyed Army Group Center in Belorussia and cut off and isolated Army Group North on the Courland Peninsula. To the south, Soviet forces launched a series of offensives into the Balkans that seized Rumania and Bulgaria, then turned north and in December encircled and laid siege to Budapest. A US bomber offensive aimed at Germany's synthetic oil plants

An Il-2M Shturmovik over Budapest. Hitler paid great attention to operations in Hungary throughout the last months of the war, and two relief operations were launched in attempts to relieve the encircled city before Budapest fell to Soviet attack in February 1945. The 5th Air Army under General Sergey Goryunov supported the 2nd Ukrainian Front throughout the campaign. (Sovfoto/Universal Images Group Editorial via Getty Images)

reduced monthly production from 175,000 tons early in the year to only 12,000 tons in September 1944. With the loss of the Ploesti oilfields to the Soviet offensive in the Balkans, Hitler's military faced severe fuel shortages. In total, 1944 had cost Germany almost one-and-a-half million casualties, and its Bulgarian, Rumanian, and Finnish allies had been driven out of the war.

The autumn of 1944 brought a measure of German recovery. In the West, logistical problems, weather, difficult terrain, and the Siegfried Line fortifications on the German border bogged down the Allied advance. In the East, the Soviet offensive across Poland had stalled at the Vistula, and German forces were able to brutally suppress the Warsaw Uprising just across the river. Hitler, searching for a means to shake the Allied alliance, marshaled all available reserves and struck the thin US line in the Ardennes Forest in December, the scene of the Wehrmacht's Blitzkrieg victory in May 1940. Within several weeks it was clear that German forces would never cross the Meuse River and threaten the port of Antwerp. The Luftwaffe had marshaled its limited fuel to support the offensive and launched Operation *Bodenplatte* (Baseplate), a surprise attack by over 800 fighters against enemy airbases in the West, in the early hours of January 1, 1945. Although it inflicted significant damage, the Luftwaffe suffered heavily during the attack, especially to its dwindling ranks of experienced pilots, while the Allies were able to rapidly replace their losses.

The Eastern Front was starved of reinforcements in early 1945 as Hitler sought success in the West. Chief of the OKH General Staff General Heinz Guderian pressed the Fuhrer to strengthen the vulnerable line on the Vistula with divisions withdrawn from the Courland Peninsula, Norway, and the Western Front, but Hitler dismissed intelligence reports of a Soviet buildup as "the greatest bluff since Ghenghis Khan." Guderian was bluntly told the Eastern Front would have to look after itself. In reality, Stalin and his General Staff were completing a massive buildup and planning nothing less than an offensive designed to break through German defenses, cross the Polish plain, and assault Berlin within weeks. Stalin planned to attack on January 20, but in response to a request from Churchill to advance the date to take pressure off the Allies in the Ardennes, agreed to begin eight days earlier despite forecasts of poor flying weather.

German Army A-4 ballistic missiles in launch position. Hitler and his leaders hoped that new technology weapons would turn the tide of war in their favor in 1944 and 1945. Many of the systems were never fielded, and those that were had less impact than anticipated. Almost all, with the exception of the Mistel Composite bomber, were used almost exclusively against the Western Allies. (Roger Viollet via Getty Images)

CHRONOLOGY

1944

Spring 1944 A renewed offensive by US heavy bombers, now escorted by long-range fighters, cripples the German fighter force.

Summer–fall 1944 A series of Allied offensives from the south, east, and west destroy whole army groups; Allied forces drive to the German frontier in the West, northern Italy in the south, and to the Vistula River in Poland. Soviet forces overrun the Balkans, capturing the Rumanian oilfields at Ploesti. US bombers attack and cripple Germany's synthetic oil plants.

December 16 The Ardennes counteroffensive begins. Hitler sends his rebuilt strategic reserve into an attack in the West, asserting that the reported buildup against his forces on the Eastern Front is a "gigantic bluff." The Ardennes offensive soon loses momentum.

1945

January 1 The Luftwaffe launches Operation *Bodenplatte* against Allied airfields in the West. The attackers achieve surprise, but they suffer heavily while the Allies rapidly replace their losses.

January 12–14 In response to a request from Churchill, Stalin advances the start of the planned Vistula–Oder offensive in the east from January 20 to the 12th. Konev's 1st Ukrainian Front attacks on the 12th and Zhukov's 1st Belarussian Front two days later. Poor weather initially limits Soviet air support by the attached 2nd and 16th Air Armies, but they soon add their weight to the assault. Soviet forces penetrate the thin German defensive lines and the advancing tank armies, supported by Shturmoviks and fighters, rapidly exploit to the west.

January 13 Chernyakovsky's 3rd Belarussian Front attacks into East Prussia supported by the 1st Air Army but encounters heavy resistance; Rokossovsky's 2nd Belarussian Front and attached 4th Air Army attack the next day to Chernyakovsky's south.

January 16 With the clearing weather, the Soviets are able to launch large numbers of sorties, overwhelming the aircraft sent up by Luftflotte 6. Chernyakovsky and Rokossovsky finally break through German resistance with heavy air support from their 1st and 4th Air Armies.

The MiG-3 was an early war design that proved unsatisfactory due to its poor performance in the low-altitude engagements common on the Eastern Front. Numbers were retained for reconnaissance, sent to Naval Aviation, or retained by the PVO Strany air defense forces where their good high-altitude capabilities were more useful. (Courtesy of the Central Museum of the Armed Forces, Moscow via www.Stavka.photos)

January 17 Warsaw is taken by Soviet and Polish forces supported by the Polish 4th Mixed Air Division. After the successful breakthrough on the Vistula, Stavka assigns more ambitious objectives to Zhukov and Konev, who are directed to seize bridgeheads over the Oder River and prepare for a February attack on Berlin.

January 17–February 2 The 1st Belarussian and 1st Ukrainian Fronts drive rapidly across Poland, led by tank armies supported by fighters and Shturmoviks overhead. Zhukov clears Lodz and drives towards the Oder River, while Konev takes Krakow and maneuvers the Germans out of the Silesian industrial zone, capturing its network of factories and mines largely intact. Soviet forces liberate Auschwitz on January 27. By February 2, the Soviets are on the Oder and less than 100km from Berlin, although VVS units have difficulty establishing forward bases and keeping up with the advance.

January 20 Although Chernyakovsky has finally broken through, reports of his initial slow progress lead the Soviet high command to divert Rokossovsky's 2nd Belarussian

Front to strike north and cut off German forces in East Prussia, leaving Zhukov's right flank uncovered.

January–February In response to the Vistula–Oder offensive, the Luftwaffe high command strips much of its force in the West and from the homeland air defenses to reinforce General Robert Ritter von Greim's Luftflotte 6, the major formation on the Eastern Front. Some 650 fighters and 100 fighter bombers arrive to augment the defense of the Oder River. The bulk of Luftwaffe air operations for the rest of the war will be on the Eastern Front.

Soviet forces are diverted by the need to encircle and eliminate a variety of cities designed as fortresses by Hitler. Konigsberg survives its first siege by the 3rd Belarussian Front, while four of Chuikov's 8th Guards Army's eight divisions take Posen on February 22.

Early February Logistical shortfalls, increased German resistance, blizzards, and warming temperatures bring the Soviet offensive to a halt on the Oder. Luftflotte 6, now reinforced, is able to operate from well-equipped permanent airbases in Germany and seizes temporary air superiority over the front. The VVS struggles to operate from improvised airfields reduced to quagmires by the thaw. Luftwaffe fighter bombers, reinforced by air defense fighters taken from the Reich, play a major role in halting the Soviet offensive and retaining German bridgeheads over the Oder at Kustrin and Frankfurt.

Marshal Zhukov, center, consults with Konev on the right during the fighting around Kursk in 1943. As the Soviet forces drove into central Europe the numerous front organizations were consolidated into fewer, more powerful units. Marshals Zhukov and Konev, the USSR's leading military commanders and fierce rivals, led the 1st Belarussian and 1st Ukrainian Fronts during the drive from Warsaw to Berlin in the last months of the war. (mil.ru/Wikimedia Commons)

February 4–10 Roosevelt, Stalin, and Churchill meet at Yalta to arrange for the conclusion of the war and to settle the division of Germany.

February 8–24 Stalin and his high command determine to clear the northern and southern flanks before launching an offensive over the Oder against Berlin. From February 8–24, Konev's 1st Ukrainian Front and its supporting 2nd Air Army conduct the Lower Silesian Operation and advance to the Neisse River southeast of Berlin. Breslau is surrounded but holds out until May 6, with the Luftwaffe struggling to land and air-drop supplies.

February 15–21 The Germans launch Operation *Sonnenwende* (Solstice) against Zhukov's weakly held northern flank, uncovered due to Rokossovsky's diversion north to cut off East Prussia. The attack is supported by elements of Greim's Luftflotte 6, but soon bogs down.

February 24–March 4 Zhukov and Rokossovsky are ordered to attack into Pomerania to secure Zhukov's northern flank. The 1st Belarussian Front reaches the Baltic coast and secures the northern Oder, while the 2nd Belarussian Front attacks north and then east towards Danzig.

March 4 The Luftwaffe restricts fighter operations against the Allied strategic bomber offensive to jets; fuel reserves are now diverted to the Eastern Front.

March 15–31 Konev makes limited gains in a second operation aimed at clearing Upper Silesia.

March 18–31 Tensions at Fuhrer conferences over holding the Kustrin bridgehead on the Oder lead to command changes. Hitler agrees to replace the ineffective Himmler as commander of Army Group Vistula with the capable General Henrici. Guderian, however, is removed as Chief of the OKH staff ten days later. Kustrin falls to a Soviet attack lasting from March 28–31.

March–April The Luftwaffe prioritizes flying supplies into isolated fortresses and striking the bridges over the Oder River. A sustained but largely unsuccessful assault on the Oder River bridges ensues, with most attacks being made by Mistel composite bombers.

March 31 The bridge at Steinau supplying Konev's 1st Ukrainian Front near Breslau is hit and severely damaged by Mistel attack.

April 1 Concerned by the increased pace of Allied advances in the West, Stalin calls his marshals to Moscow to plan the capture of Berlin.

April 2–10 Marshal Aleksandr Vasilevsky's 3rd Belarussian Front storms and captures Konigsberg, supported by a powerful aviation force including three air armies and Baltic Fleet aviation controlled by VVS commander Marshal Aleksandr Novikov. On April 7, 516 bombers of the 18th Air Army launch an unusual daylight attack, escorted by 125 fighters, to smash the city center.

April 16–18 The Berlin offensive begins. Zhukov's 1st Belarussian Front is stalled in front of Henrici's defenses on the Seelow Heights, while Konev's 1st Ukrainian Front rapidly crosses the Neisse River and exploits towards Berlin from the south over the next several days.

April 16 The Luftwaffe launches a Mistel attack that damages the rail bridge at Kustrin; sporadic attacks on the Oder bridges will continue until the end of the month.

April 19 Zhukov's 1st Belarussian Front breaks through the German defenses on the Seelow Heights with the aid of intense air support from Rudenko's 16th Air Army and the 18th Air Army's long-range bombers.

April 20 Soviet forces reach Berlin's suburbs. Rokossovsky's 2nd Belarussian Front begins its offensive to Zhukov's north, with his attached 4th Air Army playing a major role as his artillery is still in the process of moving forward after the conclusion of the Pomeranian operation.

April 24 Luftflotte 6 commander General von Greim is called to Hitler's bunker, promoted to field marshal, and appointed commander of the Luftwaffe. Elements of the German 9th and 4th Panzer Armies are surrounded to the southeast of Berlin and neutralized by sustained Soviet air attacks by elements from the 2nd and 16th Air Armies over the next week.

April 24–25 Berlin is struck by 111 bombers from the 18th Air Army on the 24th, followed the next day by a raid by 563 bombers.

VVS fighters at a field airstrip with camouflage netting covering some of the parking area. The Soviet military placed a major emphasis on *maskirovka* – camouflage, concealment, and deception – activities. (Nik Cornish at www.Stavka.photos)

April 25 Berlin is fully encircled by Zhukov's and Konev's forces. Elements of the Soviet 5th Guards Army and US 1st Army meet on the Elbe River near Torgau. The 16th Air Army launches two massive attacks on German positions in Berlin, the first with 949 aircraft (463 bombers, 486 fighters) and the second with 589 (267 bombers, 322 fighters).

April 28 Tempelhof Airfield on the outskirts of Berlin is taken by Soviet forces and rapidly used by VVS fighter units. The Luftwaffe is reduced to scattered supply drops to Berlin and landings on improvised road strips by light liaison planes.

April 30 Hitler commits suicide and troops of the Soviet 150th Rifle Division raise the Red Banner over the Reichstag.

May 2 The Soviets storm the Reich Chancellery and the Berlin garrison surrenders.

May 4 German forces in northwest Germany, the Netherlands, and Denmark surrender.

May 6 Breslau surrenders.

May 8–9 German forces surrender throughout Europe; the last scattered engagements between Luftwaffe and Soviet aircraft take place on the 8th and 9th.

May 11 Fighting dies out in Prague.

July 17 The Potsdam Conference begins.

ATTACKER'S CAPABILITIES

The VVS on the brink of victory

Stalin famously called the Il-2M Shturmovik as necessary to the Red Army "as air and bread," and its low-level cannon, bomb, and rocket attacks on German forces were the critical component of the VVS's air offensive doctrine. (Courtesy of the Central Museum of the Armed Forces, Moscow via www.Stavka.photos)

The Soviet Air Force suffered shattering losses in the first weeks of the war with Germany, and during 1942 had only been able to battle the qualitatively superior Luftwaffe by throwing in thousands of aircraft and poorly trained pilots to hold the line. The tide began to turn in 1943 as improved Soviet aircraft and more capable pilots began to grind down their outnumbered and overextended opponents. The USSR produced 28,984 combat aircraft in 1943 and 32,649 the next year, with a heavy emphasis on fighters and Il-2M Shturmoviks. By 1945, the VVS was a massive force ready to provide powerful support to Red Army offensives. In January, VVS frontal aviation consisted of 14,046 combat aircraft, 12,868 of which were newer models, including 3,330 bombers, 4,171 ground attack aircraft, 5,810 fighters, and 735 reconnaissance and artillery spotting aircraft. French and Czech squadrons and a Polish air division were integrated into the force structure, and 200 now-allied Rumanian and Bulgarian aircraft flew with the Soviets south of the Carpathians. Soviet Naval Aviation aircraft operated on the coastal axes, and the long-range bomber force, reorganized in December 1944 as the 18th Air Army, operated a small number of four-engine bombers and over 700 medium bombers. The Stavka high command held an additional 575 aircraft in several reserve air corps, ready to be dispatched to the front for major offensives.

The air offensive

The story of the VVS in the last years of the war is essentially the story of the air offensive – the concentrated application of Soviet air power to support breakthrough and exploitation operations by ground forces. During the entire war, 46.5 percent of air army combat sorties were attacks on enemy forces on or near the battlefield, and a large portion of the remainder were escort operations by covering fighter units or bomber raids on targets close to the front. Unlike Western air forces, strategic bombing and deep interdiction operations were extremely rare and there was little effort to conduct sustained attacks on enemy airbases or fighter

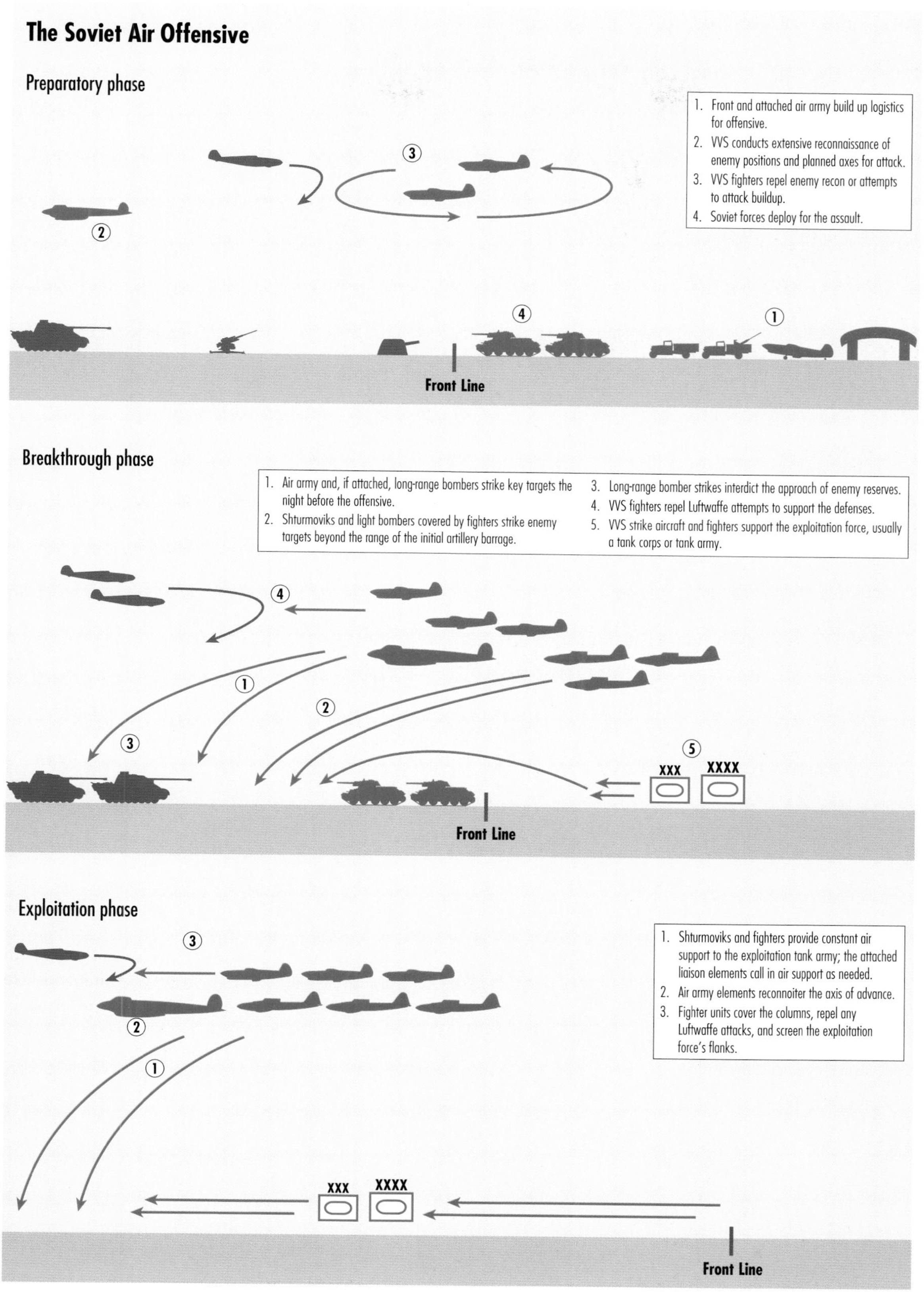
The Soviet Air Offensive
Preparatory phase
1. Front and attached air army build up logistics for offensive.
2. VVS conducts extensive reconnaissance of enemy positions and planned axes for attack.
3. VVS fighters repel enemy recon or attempts to attack buildup.
4. Soviet forces deploy for the assault.
Front Line
Breakthrough phase
1. Air army and, if attached, long-range bombers strike key targets the night before the offensive.
2. Shturmoviks and light bombers covered by fighters strike enemy targets beyond the range of the initial artillery barrage.
3. Long-range bomber strikes interdict the approach of enemy reserves.
4. VVS fighters repel Luftwaffe attempts to support the defenses.
5. VVS strike aircraft and fighters support the exploitation force, usually a tank corps or tank army.
XXX
XXXX
Front Line
Exploitation phase
1. Shturmoviks and fighters provide constant air support to the exploitation tank army; the attached liaison elements call in air support as needed.
2. Air army elements reconnoiter the axis of advance.
3. Fighter units cover the columns, repel any Luftwaffe attacks, and screen the exploitation force's flanks.
XXX
XXXX
Front Line

ABOVE THE SOVIET AIR OFFENSIVE

A formation of Pe-2 light bombers. Less well-known that the Shturmovik, the Pe-2 equipped most of the frontal aviation bomber regiments during the war. The aircraft was extremely versatile, serving in level- and dive-bombing roles, and as the dominant VVS late-war reconnaissance aircraft. (Courtesy of the Central Museum of the Armed Forces, Moscow via www.Stavka.photos)

sweeps in pursuit of theater-wide air superiority. The heavily armored Il-2M Shturmovik ground attack aircraft and the bombers of the air armies were primarily used as flying artillery to attack targets near the front that were out of the range of the ground forces' heavy guns. Soviet fighter operations were closely tied to escorting the ground attack and bomber force. The VVS conducted Otoniki free hunter fighter operations to seek out and engage enemy aircraft, as well as attacks on enemy airfields but on a much smaller scale. This allowed the Luftwaffe to remain a force in being able to contest air control on select sectors even while heavily outnumbered in the last years of the war.

By 1943, the VVS doctrine for the support of ground operations was termed the "air offensive." Each Soviet Front was typically supported by a dedicated VVS frontal aviation air army, whose operations were dictated by the front commander's plans for breakthrough and exploitation. Aviation was massed to support the fronts selected for major offensives; in 1942–43, 70–75 percent of VVS airpower was allocated to major offensives, and in the last two years of the war the percentage rose to 90–95. The air armies involved were heavily reinforced by the addition of reserve air corps dispatched by the high command. The air offensive would begin with a preparatory phase involving extensive photo reconnaissance flights over the area selected for the breakthrough, while fighter screens intercepted any Luftwaffe efforts to disrupt the build up of Soviet ground forces and logistics. The Soviets favored the use of *maskirovka* camouflage and deception operations, with the VVS establishing decoy airfields, mockups of fighters and bombers, and simulated radio traffic to deceive the Germans as to the primary axes of attack, and ideally lead them to expend effort attacking false positions. Night bombing attacks against select targets were usually launched in the early hours of an offensive. As the assault began, fighters would defend the Shturmovik ground attack aircraft and light bombers as they launched low-level attacks against targets outside the range of the attacker's artillery, including strongpoints, reserve units, and supporting artillery positions. If assigned to support the offensive, the medium bombers of long-range aviation would hit enemy headquarters, reserves, and some rail junctions to isolate the battlefield. These long-range aviation attacks, although at times characterized as deep interdiction by the Soviets, were generally still within a few kilometers of the front line. As the Soviet forces broke through, fighters and Shturmoviks directly attached to the exploiting tank and mechanized forces would strike targets ahead of the advancing columns and protect their flanks.

Overall Soviet organization

The USSR's aviation assets were operated by five organizations. The Soviet Air Force, the VVS, was the primary aviation element and was almost totally dedicated to supporting ground force operations at the front. Until December 1944, the few available four-engine bombers, along with larger numbers of two-engine medium bombers, were formed into a separate command, Long-Range Aviation (LRA), and directly subordinated to the Stavka high command. In December, LRA was reorganized as the 18th Air Army and placed under VVS control. The Soviet Navy had its own naval aviation force, VVS-VMF, with each of its four fleets controlling a number of aviation fighter, ground attack, bomber, and reconnaissance regiments. Apart from small numbers of maritime patrol aircraft, Soviet naval aviation predominantly used the same aircraft as the VVS and operated from land airfields on coastal axes. A separate organization, Forces of Air Defense (PVO), controlled fighter units along with radars, searchlights, and antiaircraft guns organized to defend Soviet cities, but was not heavily engaged in the 1945 battles. Finally, the civilian air fleet (GVF) was dedicated to the war effort as of 1941 and contributed transport aircraft.

Command and control

Soviet aviation command and control improved steadily during the war. As air–ground integration was paramount, VVS air army commanders and staffs were typically collocated with the front commanders their aircraft supported. Similarly, aviation staffs were assigned to combined arms army or tank army headquarters, and aviation liaison elements were attached to exploiting tank and mechanized brigades once the front was broken to call in aviation support as needed. Ground and air planning was fully integrated and addressed targets, aircraft lanes, and bomb lines. Many VVS aircraft lacked radios or had only receiver sets early in the war, but from 1943 fighters were equipped with full RSI-3 or RSI-4, and bombers with RSB-3bis radio sets. Soviet commanders were now able to use their networks of Redut and Pegmantit radars and RAF, RAT, and RSB radio relay stations to orchestrate air activities and vector aircraft against enemy activity. Particularly large-scale operations involving multiple VVS air armies were often controlled by a special staff group drawn from Air Force high command and led by the VVS commander-in-chief, Marshal Aleksandr Novikov.

Pilot and crew training

Pilot and crew training had been a major VVS weakness during the first years of the war. The pressure to keep forward units manned with aircrew despite the heavy losses in 1941 and 1942 led to pilots arriving at front-line units with very few hours in their logbooks. The trainees mostly practiced taking off and landing, and any maneuvering or gunnery skills would have to be picked up with the unit should the novice pilot survive long enough. By the later period of the war, the situation had reversed, with large numbers of experienced

Pilot mission planning before a sortie. VVS leadership and command and control improved steadily throughout the war, and by 1945 was extremely capable of orchestrating its fighter, ground attack, and bomber forces in support of Red Army offensives. (Courtesy of the Central Museum of the Armed Forces, Moscow via www.Stavka.photos)

VVS fighter pilots facing a Luftwaffe fighter arm primarily manned by novice pilots with only a few hours of training and more of a danger to themselves than the enemy when aloft.

Aircraft roles and capabilities

Fighters

After its huge losses during the first months of the war, the Soviets battled the Luftwaffe by fielding large numbers of fighters and poorly trained pilots, but the flexible finger-four-*schwarm* tactics of the veteran Luftwaffe pilots, flying Bf 109 fighters superior to the VVS's I-16s, I-153s, LaGG-3s, and MiG-3s, inflicted heavy losses. By 1943, the tide in the air started to turn as improved Soviet fighter designs joined the force and, by 1945, VVS fighter regiments were equipped with the latest Yak-3s, Yak-9s, La-5FNs, and La-7s. Over 36,000 Yak fighters of all models were produced during the war, 16,769 of them various models of the Yak-9. Most Yak-9s were armed with a 20mm cannon and two 12.7mm machine guns and were able to deliver a 200kg bomb load. A total of 3,921 of the later Yak-9P/U versions were produced through the summer of 1945. The Yak-3 was a pure interceptor with excellent dogfighting capabilities below 5,000 meters, where most aerial combat on the Eastern Front took place. The Yak-3 was one of the most maneuverable fighters of the war and had one of the highest kill-to-loss ratios of any Soviet fighter. When the famous French-manned Normandie-Niemen Squadron was offered its pick of fighter types, it chose the Yak-3, and after the war returned to France with the surviving 42 aircraft. The Lavochkin La-5FN gave Soviet pilots an aircraft able to match the Bf 109 G in 1943. Losses of all La-5 types fell from 1,460 in 1943 to 825 in 1944. With the La-7, the VVS had a fighter superior to anything it would face on the Eastern Front, and about 400 had joined the VVS at the front in early 1945. The VVS flew numbers of P-39 Aircobras received via lend-lease until the end of the war, being the recipient of almost half of the aircraft produced. The aircraft was withdrawn from service in the West due to its poor high-altitude performance, but was favored by the Soviets for its firepower and maneuverability in the low-level air engagements typical of the air war on the Eastern Front. As was the case with most Western aircraft, Soviet pilots liked the P-39's roomy cockpit and excellent radios. The second-highest-ranking VVS ace, Aleksandr Pokryshkin, scored most of his 59 victories flying the aircraft that the Soviets dubbed the Kobra.

Ground attack

Soviet ground attack units flew the legendary Il-2M Shturmovik. Designed by Ilyushin in 1939 for low-level attack runs, the aircraft had an armored shell as an integral part of the airframe protecting the pilot, engine, and fuel tanks, and from 1944 the use of metal wings made the aircraft even more survivable. Over 36,000 of all versions left the factories. Soviet aircraft weaponry was excellent during the war, and the Il-2M was typically outfitted with two ShVAK 20mm cannon and two ShKAS 7.62mm machine guns. Initial models only carried a pilot and lost heavily to enemy attack from behind, but a rear gunner manning a UBT 12.7mm machine gun was added in the Il-2M version that entered production in September 1942. Il-2Ms used RS-82 rockets and could carry and deliver 280 PTAB cluster bombs in its internal bomb bays, each carrying a high-explosive antitank warhead able to penetrate the upper armor on German tanks. Il-2Ms often employed a circle formation when on the attack, with each aircraft able to protect the tail of the one ahead and allowing Il-2Ms to peel off one-by-one to execute attacks on the ground target below.

In October 1944, production of the Il-10 – the Il-2's replacement – began and large numbers joined the VVS in February 1945. The Il-10 strongly resembled its predecessor but was an all-metal design, and with a top speed of 550km/h at 2,300 meters was some 140km/h faster than the Il-2. It carried a heavier armament, with two 7.62mm machine guns

Soviet Yak fighters. By 1945, the VVS was almost completely equipped with modern fighters, including the Yak-3, -9 and La-5FN and La-7, that matched or outclassed their Luftwaffe counterparts in most key performance criteria. (Courtesy of the Central Museum of the Armed Forces, Moscow via www.Stavka.photos)

and up to four 23mm cannon, along with the rear gunner's 12.7mm heavy machine gun. A total of 785 Il-10s were produced before the end of the war, the figure rising to almost 5,000 with postwar production.

Light bombers

The USSR started the war with a force largely composed of obsolete bombers that were slow, poorly armed, and equipped with antiquated avionics. The exception was the Pe-2, an extremely versatile aircraft originally designed to serve as a twin-engine fighter but soon used in dive-bomber, level bomber, and reconnaissance roles. Overshadowed by the Shturmovik, the Pe-2 became the dominant Soviet light tactical bomber of the war, able to carry 1,000kg of bombs, rockets, and armed with mixes of 20mm cannon and 7.62mm or 12.7mm machine guns. In total, 11,247 Pe-2s were produced. The Tu-2 was a capable four-seat light bomber that made a less profound contribution to the Soviet war effort. Development was lengthy, and the Pe-2 remained in the force in large numbers even as the Tu-2 began to be fielded. The production version, known as the Tu-2S, finally entered service in 1944, and 1,100 were produced during the war, equipping several air army bomber divisions during the last months of the conflict. Another 1,427 were produced after the end of the war. The Tu-2 was typically used for level bombing and had a maximum 1,500kg bomb load. The bomber was fast, with a maximum speed of 550km/h, and carried mixes of 20mm and 23mm cannon and machine guns.

Soviet light bombers were typically used against targets on or near the front line. Bombing was during daylight hours, with only a few elite crews assigned night missions. The bomber force lacked precision navigation aids and tended to launch their attacks based on landmark identification. Pe-2s could dive at a sharp angle, Tu-2s at angles not exceeding 60 degrees, but both types more typically used level bombing. At times, dive-bombing attacks were used against enemy antiaircraft positions to clear the way for larger level bombing formations. Bomber raids varied with the importance of the target, with divisional-sized raids of up to 50–100 bombers for critical missions.

Long-range bomber force

The USSR launched small-scale strategic bombing raids against a variety of targets, including Berlin and the Ploesti oilfields, in 1941. Moscow organized its four-engine and medium

Soviet Shturmovik Tactics

Soviet air offensive doctrine placed the primary focus on the execution of strikes by Shturmovik ground attack and bomber aircraft on enemy ground force targets at or near the front line; most fighter operations were to protect the strike aircraft from enemy attack. Typically, one fighter was in the escort for every Shturmovik. The Shturmovik formation (C) was covered by an assault formation (D) consisting of a number of para- lead and wingman-pair formations weaving 450 to 900m above. The mission of the assault formation was to identify and engage enemy fighters, diving on them out of the sun or clouds to achieve surprise before they could reach the Shturmoviks. Close escort (B) flew 100 to 300m above and slightly behind the Il-2Ms, and its mission was to engage any Luftwaffe fighters that got through the assault formation. If no enemy was encountered, VVS fighters might be used to strafe enemy ground targets. If additional fighters were available, escorts could be positioned in front of (E), above (A), or slightly below (F) the ground attack formation. In no circumstances would VVS fighters be allowed to leave the Shturmoviks.

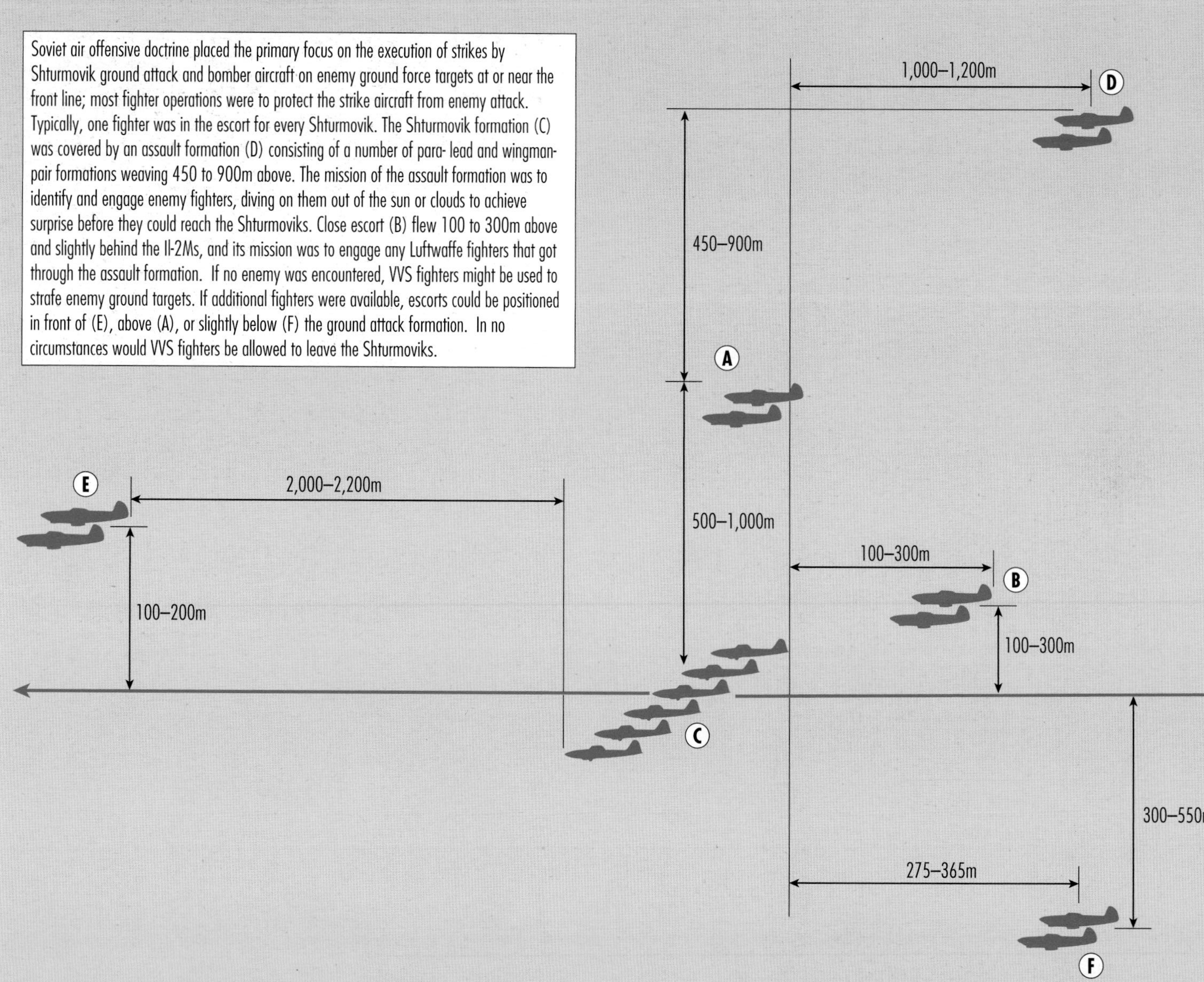

OPPOSITE FIGHTER ESCORT OF SHTURMOVIK GROUND ATTACK AIRCRAFT

two-engine bombers into a special force designated Long-Range Aviation and directly controlled by the high command until December 1944. After suffering huge losses in daylight operations in 1941, LRA bombers were confined to night raids, typically against rail yards or German headquarters and reserves relatively close to the front line. On 6 December 1944, LRA's status as a separate force was removed, and it was reformed as the 18th Air Army and subordinated to Novikov and the VVS headquarters. The formal rationale was to improve long-range bomber integration with ground operations, but the actual reason was Stalin's fury at discovering that LRA raids on Helsinki intended to drive Finland from the war earlier in the year had inflicted almost no damage.

The Soviet long-range bomber force included small numbers of TB-3 and Pe-8 four-engine bombers but was overwhelmingly equipped with two-engine medium Il-4s, B-25s, and A-20s. The Soviets also converted some C-47 transports received via lend-lease, designated the Li-2, to serve as night bombers. The TB-3 was a prewar design and officially withdrawn from active service in 1939. Nevertheless, of the 818 produced, 516 were still available when the war began and were soon pressed into daylight bombing operations, where they suffered heavy losses. The aircraft continued to serve throughout the war as a night bomber and general purpose and paratroop transport, with ten in the operational force in 1945. The Pe-8 was a more modern prewar design, but although production continued into the war years, only a total of 93 left the factories. Losses to enemy action and other causes led to the Pe-8 being removed from the bomber force in 1944, and the 18th Air Army's 45th Heavy Bomber Division transitioned to the B-25 Mitchell medium bomber.

Pe-2 light bombers preparing for a bombing run. The Pe-2 equipped many of the bomber units controlled by VVS air armies. In April 1945, six of the ten bomber divisions assigned to Rudenko's 16th Air Army were equipped with Pe-2s. (Nik Cornish at www.Stavka.photos)

The mainstay of Golovanov's Long-Range Aviation force was the Il-4 medium bomber. The Il-4 had a crew of four and carried 2,500kg of bombs internally, and often had an additional 1,000kg mounted on its wings. (From the fonds of the RGAKFD in Krasnogorsk via www.Stavka.photos)

The mainstay of the Soviet long-range bomber force was the Il-4 twin-engine medium bomber, a versatile platform that served throughout the war with over 5,000 produced. Some Il-4s were adapted to serve as torpedo bombers for Soviet Naval Aviation. The Il-4 was considered reliable and tough, but its light defensive armament had contributed to heavy losses during daylight raids in 1941, and it was relegated thereafter to night operations. Lend-lease bombers included the A-20 Havoc, and were provided in large numbers to the USSR. Most A-20s were G models developed in the US with heavy cannon and machine guns in the nose for low-level strafing runs, but due to losses from German Flak, the Soviets typically replaced the nose guns with a glass front to allow for level bombing runs. The B-25 Mitchell, also provided for the Soviet bomber force, had the best range and payload of the three.

The 18th Air Army confined its operations almost completely to the hours of night and faced challenges navigating to and hitting its targets. The bombers flew in a loose stream formed as they took off in sequence, and there was little systematic effort to mark the target, although there was some use of flare cascades. In 1945, of 14,979 18th Air Army sorties, 7,927 were for troop support, 5,251 hit railways – mostly close to the front – 1,731 were against ports, and 70 against enemy airfields. Targets farther from the front line assigned to the 18th Air Army were often rail yards, struck to hinder the movement of German reserves and reinforcements.

The commanders

Soviet airmen were led by proven and capable commanders in 1945. Marshal Aleksandr Novikov had originally joined the Red Army as an infantryman in 1919, fought in the Civil War, and only moved to the VVS in 1933. Purged and rehabilitated in the late 1930s, he led the Soviet air forces in the Leningrad Military District during the Russo-Finnish Winter War of 1939–40 and during the 1941 German invasion. Appointed to command the VVS in April 1942, Novikov immediately initiated a series of reforms to improve performance, most critically ordering the creation of air armies to centralize aviation operations in support of every front. Novikov led VVS operations at Stalingrad and in every major engagement afterwards, and was awarded both the Hero of the Soviet Union and the US Legion of Merit.

Marshal A. Ye. Golovanov commanded the Soviet's dedicated bomber force, the 18th Air Army. Golovanov began the war personally leading some of the USSR's early small-scale strategic bombing raids. He was appointed to lead the Long-Range Aviation force on its formation in February 1942 and was promoted to marshal rank in August 1943 at the age of 39 – the youngest marshal in the Soviet Union. Golovanov continued to command the bomber force after Stalin downgraded it to air army status and placed it under control of the VVS.

The air armies supporting the final assault across Poland were all led by experienced officers. General Sergey I. Rudenko joined the Red Army after the Civil War in 1923 and commanded an air squadron in 1932. He commanded the 31st Mixed Air Division at the start of the war and was appointed to command the 16th Air Army upon its formation in October 1942. General Stepan A. Krasovsky had served during World War I as an NCO and commanded a Red Army air detachment fighting against Admiral Kolchak's Whites. Krasovsky commanded the North Caucasus Military District's aviation forces at the onset of Operation *Barbarossa* and led the 17th Air Army during the Stalingrad campaign. In March 1943, Krasovsky took over the 2nd Air Army and led it through the rest of the war. Konstantin A. Vershinin had joined the Red Army upon the outbreak of the Revolution in 1917 and attended the Zukhovsky Air Force Academy in 1929. Vershinin commanded the 4th Air Army throughout the war. General Timofey T. Khryukin commanded the 1st Air Army during the campaign. Khryukin was active in the years before the war, serving as a bomber pilot in Spain and subsequently leading a squadron of SB Tupelov bombers for the Chinese Nationalist Air Force against the Japanese. After the German invasion, he organized the aviation defenses for the Murmansk and Kirov Railways, critical for the movement of Allied supplies delivered to Arctic ports, and then commanded the 8th Air Army during the Stalingrad campaign. Following a promotion in July 1944, Khryukin took command of the 1st Air Army.

One of the great commanders of World War II, Aleksandr Novikov instituted organizational changes that magnified VVS combat power in 1942, and led Soviet air armies in all of the major actions throughout the end of the war. (Unknown/ Wikimedia Commons)

The order of battle

The critical Soviet frontal aviation organization was the air army – the *Vozdushnya Armii* (VA). In 1941, the VVS was organized with a major percentage of its resources directly controlled by Soviet combined arms army commanders, dispersing its assets. The new air force commander appointed by Stalin in 1942, Aleksandr Novikov, created air armies to centralize all bomber, ground attack, and fighter aircraft under a unified air army headquarters. An air army would normally support each Soviet front, a formation analogous to a German or Allied army group. The air army controlled various mixes of air corps, divisions, and often small numbers of independent regiments as well as airfield, maintenance, signals support, and antiaircraft units. Units and equipment varied, but an average late war air army could include 1,400 or more aircraft, 41,000 officers and men, and 3,500–4,000 trucks. The VVS ultimately formed 18 air armies during the war, along with over 175 air divisions and large numbers of separate regiments.

The VVS order of battle contained a number of foreign units during the last years of the war. French volunteers formed the heavily publicized Normandie Squadron in 1942, which expanded to regimental strength and was given the honorific Normandie-Niemen

The famous Normandie-Niemen Squadron was formed by Free French pilots who flew from Syria to the Soviet Union earlier in the war and were offered by de Gaul to Stalin. Later formed into a regiment, the squadron operated Yak-3s and operated over East Prussia and Konigsberg in 1945 as part of the 1st Air Army. The photo shows the Yak-3s of the regiment on their return to France in June 1945. (AFP via Getty Images)

title in October 1944. The unit was ultimately credited with 273 confirmed kills and returned to France with its surviving 42 Yak-3 fighters after the fall of Berlin. Polish airmen manned the 1st Warsaw Fighter Regiment with Yak-1s and 2nd Krakow Night Bomber Air Regiment with Po-2s in early 1944, and the force expanded to form the Polish 4th Mixed Air Division with the 1st Fighter, 2nd Light Bomber, and 3rd Ground Attack Regiments by the end of the year. By 1945, the force expanded into the 1st Polish Mixed Air Corps, and later formed the nucleus for the Cold War communist Polish Air Force. Similarly, Czech pilots formed an air regiment in July 1944 and expanded to the 1st Mixed Air Division that operated with Konev's forces during the drive to Prague in the last days of the war. In the Balkans, after leaving the Axis alliance, Rumania contributed an air corps to operate with the 2nd Ukrainian Front.

By 1945, an air army's subordinate air divisions and corps were usually organized as pure fighter, ground attack, or bomber units rather than the unsuccessful mixed-type formations employed earlier in the war. The basic VVS organization was the regiment, with full-strength fighter and ground attack regiments consisting of three squadrons and totaling 36 line and four headquarters aircraft, and bomber regiments of 27 aircraft. Three or four regiments were in each division, and divisions either subordinated directly to the air army headquarters or to an air corps. Air corps typically controlled two and sometimes three divisions. To give Stavka the ability to rapidly influence the battlefield, the high command directly controlled varying numbers of reserve air corps that would be assigned to augment air armies on key axes as needed. By the end of the war, 30 reserve corps of the Supreme High Command had been formed, comprising seven bomber, 11 ground attack, and 12 fighter corps.

The Soviet air offensive was focused on direct support to ground forces operations. Fighters covered attacking Shturmoviks and bombers and were often additionally tasked to strafe and bomb ground targets themselves. (Courtesy of the Central Museum of the Armed Forces, Moscow via www.Stavka.photos)

VVS Order of Battle, January 1945

Vistula–Oder Operation
1st Belarussian Front – Marshal G. K. Zhukov
16th Air Army – General S. I. Rudenko
6th and 13th Fighter Corps
6th Assault Air Corps
1st Guards, 282nd and 286th Fighter Divisions
2nd and 11th Guards Ground Attack Divisions
183rd and 221st Bomber Divisions
9th Guards Night Bomber Division
16th Independent Reconnaissance Regiment
980th Independent Fire-Adjustment Reconnaissance Regiment
Additional elements assigned to the 16th Air Army from 6th Air Army and Stavka Reserve
5th Guards Fighter Corps
9th Assault Air Corps
183rd Bomber Division
242nd Night Bomber Division
1st Guards Fighter Division
72nd Independent Fire-Adjustment Reconnaissance Regiment
2nd Ukrainian Front – Marshal I. S. Konev
2nd Air Army – General S. A. Krasovsky
6th Guards, 2nd, and 5th Fighter Corps
2nd and 5th Guards and 3rd Assault Air Corps
2nd Guards and 4th Bomber Corps
208th Night Bomber Division
98th and 193rd Independent Reconnaissance Regiments
118th Independent Fire-Adjustment Reconnaissance Regiment

East Prussian Operation
3rd Belarussian Front – Marshal I. D. Chernyakovsky
1st Air Army – General T. T. Khryukin
129th, 130th, 240th, 303rd, and 330th Fighter Divisions
9th Fighter Regiment
1st Guards, 217th, 282nd, and 311th Assault Air Divisions
6th and 276th Bomber Divisions
213th Night Bomber Division
10th Air Reconnaissance Regiment
117th, and 151st Fire Correction Reconnaissance Regiments
2nd Belarussian Front – Marshal K. K. Rokossovsky
4th Air Army – General K. A. Vershinin
8th Fighter Corps
229th, 269th, 309th, and 329th Fighter Divisions
4th Assault Air Corps
230th, 233rd, 260th, and 332nd Assault Air Divisions
5th Bomber Division
325th Night Bomber Division
164th Independence Reconnaissance Regiment
18th Air Army – Marshal A. Ye. Golovanov
1st Guards, 2nd, 3rd, and 4th Bomber Corps
45th Heavy Bomber Division
56th Fighter Division

VVS Order of Battle, April 1945

Berlin Offensive
2nd Belarussian Front – Marshal K. K. Rokossovsky
4th Air Army – General K. A. Vershinin
4th Assault Air Corps
230th, 233rd, 260th, and 332nd Assault Air Divisions
5th Bomber Corps
8th Fighter Corps
229th, 269th, 309th, and 329th Fighter Divisions
325th Night Bomber Division
164th Independent Reconnaissance Regiment
1st Belarussian Front – Marshal G. K. Zhukov
16th Air Army – General S. I. Rudenko
1st and 3rd Guards, 6th and 13th Air Fighter Corps
1st Guards, 240th, 282nd, and 286th Air Fighter Divisions
6th and 9th Ground Attack Corps
2nd and 11th Guards Ground Attack Divisions
3rd and 6th Bomber Corps
188th and 221st Bomber Divisions
9th Guards and 242nd Air Night Bomber Divisions
4th Polish Mixed Air Division
18th Air Army – Marshal A. Ye. Golovanov
1st, 2nd, 3rd, and 4th Guards, and 29th Air Bomber Corps
45th Heavy Air Bomber Division
56th Air Fighter Division
1st Ukrainian Front – Marshal I. S. Konev
2nd Air Army – General S. A. Krasovsky
1st and 2nd Guards, and 3rd Attack Air Corps
6th Guards and 4th Bomber Corps
2nd, 5th, and 6th Guards Air Fighter Corps
208th Air Night Aviation Division
193rd Guards Reconnaissance Regiment

DEFENDER'S CAPABILITIES

The last of the Luftwaffe

The preeminent Luftwaffe *schlachtflieger* (fighter bomber) of the last several years of the war was the Fw 190. The F-8, pictured here, had two 20mm MG 151/20 cannon on the wings and two 13mm MG 131 machine guns on the front cowling. The aircraft was fitted to carry bombs on the centerline and wings. Some versions of the Fw 190 used in 1945 had infantry 81mm or 88mm antitank rockets on the aircraft for improved capabilities against enemy armor. (Bettmann via Getty Images)

The Luftwaffe was under immense pressure in January 1945, but it would fight until the end of the war, almost to the last drop of fuel and until its last airfields were overrun. Germany had at last focused on increasing aircraft production in 1944, and a record 3,821 aircraft left the factories that September alone. The production surge was, however, at least two years too late and never overcame the heavy attrition suffered fighting the Allies on multiple fronts. Germany had a force of just over 4,500 serviceable aircraft in early 1945, roughly the same

Even with the late-war surge in German fighter production, the Luftwaffe struggled to maintain its numbers due to the demands of several major fronts and heavy attrition both at the hands of the Western Allies and the Soviets. (Courtesy of the Central Museum of the Armed Forces, Moscow via www.Stavka.photos)

number as it had in the early years of the war, but the Luftwaffe faced over 13,000 Soviet aircraft alone, plus the thousands more flown by the USAAF and RAF.

The surge in aircraft production was in any case negated by the shortage of fuel. The loss of the Rumanian oilfields during 1944 and the USAAF bomber offensive against the synthetic oil plants rapidly reduced reserves. The Luftwaffe had consumed 90,000,000 gallons of fuel in June 1944, but would only have 95,000,000 gallons available for the remainder of the war. The shortage had a particularly devastating impact on an already-stressed Luftwaffe training program. Germany had struggled for years to produce enough pilots and aircraft to keep up with losses, and the length of the program was steadily reduced. With the 1944 fuel shortages, training flight hours were restricted further, and Luftwaffe trainees usually arrived at operational units with no hours in the aircraft they would fly in combat. As the Western Allies closed on the Rhine in late 1944, US and British fighter sweeps over Germany began to intercept and down training flights and attack training airfields with increased frequency.

Luftwaffe order of battle, January and April 1945

	January 10, 1945	April 9, 1945
Day fighters	1,462	1,305
Night fighters	808	485
Ground attack	613	712
Night-harassment aircraft	302	215
Multi-engine bombers	294	37
Anti-shipping aircraft	83	–
Long-range reconnaissance aircraft	176	143
Short-range reconnaissance and army cooperation aircraft	293	309
Coastal aircraft	60	45
Transport aircraft	269	10
KG 200 (Special operations)	206	70
Total	4,566	3,331

Aircraft, roles, and capabilities

Fighters

The early years of the war in the East saw well-trained and experienced Luftwaffe pilots flying superior aircraft shoot down large numbers of their Soviet opponents. Unlike their Allied counterparts, Luftwaffe pilots flew without rotation throughout the war, and successful veterans might total 500 to even 1,000 or more sorties. A number of these *Experte* pilots would amass scores of a hundred or more kills. By 1943, however, the Soviets were able to field not only a force that continued to outnumber the Luftwaffe, but one with improved aircraft and better-trained pilots. By 1944, the VVS had achieved front-wide air superiority. The Luftwaffe was reduced to acting as a fire brigade, with its limited assets shifted from one section of the front to another as the Red Army launched offensive after offensive. 1945 saw dwindling numbers of *Experte* pilots still capable of increasing their scores, but the mass of Luftwaffe pilots were ill-prepared for survival in the brutal, low-level air-to-air combats typical of the Eastern Front.

The Luftwaffe still operated large numbers of late-production models of the Bf 109; in January 1945, Luftflotte 6's two fighter groups in Poland were completely equipped with 109s.

The Yak-3 was an excellent dogfighter, and superior to both the Bf 109 and Fw 190A at altitudes below 5,000 meters. German airmen were instructed to avoid engaging Yak fighters that lacked oil coolers under the nose – Yak-3s – at low altitudes. (Sovfoto/ Universal Images Group via Getty Images)

The Bf 109 first flew in combat during the Spanish Civil War and dominated the skies over Europe from 1939–42, but was now outclassed by the latest Soviet and Western fighters. The airframe could not accept an engine larger that the Daimler Benz DB 605 that outfitted the G models, so no major improvement in performance was possible, and the latest Allied fighters – including the VVS's Yak-3s and Yak-9s, La-5FNs, and La-7s – were equal or superior in all performance areas. Some Bf 109 G-10s were specially outfitted for high-altitude dogfighting to cover other aircraft trying to strike the USAAF massed bomber formations. One in four of the Bf 109s operating in 1945 were K-4 models, lightened to increase speed and rate of climb.

The Focke Wulf Fw 190 began service on the Eastern Front in 1942 and provided the Luftwaffe with an excellent fighter for low-level dogfights with their VVS opponents. The Fw 190 was rugged and able to operate in the primitive airfield conditions typical in the East, maneuverable, and provided a stable gun platform. In 1944, the Fw 190D or Dora version was fitted with a Junkers Jumo 213 in-line engine that provided extra power and allowed the aircraft to meet the newer Allied Spitfire XIV, P-51D Mustang, Yak-3, and La-7 on equal terms. The Focke Wulf Ta 152 version, the culmination of the basic 190 design, had a lengthened wing for better performance and a high maximum speed of 760km/h, but few were able to join the force before the end of the war.

A specialized Fw 190, designated the *Sturmbock* (battering ram), was developed to increase the ability of German fighters to bring down US heavy bombers. The Sturmbock received heavier protection around the cockpit and ammunition boxes and carried two 30mm cannon rather than the 190's normal 20mm versions. Massed formations of the fighters were intended to close on US bombers from the rear and attack with the cannons which, despite their slow rate of fire, could do significant damage at close range. With 400lb of additional weight, however, the Sturmbock was at a major disadvantage in any air-to-air combat situation when numbers were rushed to the Eastern Front in 1945.

There was much hope that advanced technology aircraft, especially the Me 262 jet fighter, would allow the Luftwaffe to wrest air superiority back from the enemy. The Me 262 could achieve 870km/h and carried four 30mm cannon, giving it speed and firepower superior to any Allied opponent. The Jumo 004 engines, however, were prone to failures and fires, delaying the full production of the fighter for months. By January 1945, around 1,000 had been built but only about 60 were with front-line units, and these were in fighter bomber or reconnaissance roles, and fires and accidents were still common. In April 1945, about 1,200 Me 262s had been accepted by the Luftwaffe, but issues with aircraft reliability, pilot training, fuel shortages, and continuous US and RAF fighter raids on the jet bases reduced their effectiveness. The largest number to ever fly in one day, 57, engaged US bombers on 7 April. Until the last days of the fighting for Berlin, Me 262s were used to engage Western bomber formations and rarely met Soviet opponents. The Me 163 rocket-propelled fighter had an even higher speed than the 262, but with a range of just 25 miles could only function as a point-defense asset.

Fighter bombers

Direct support to ground forces was the key mission for the Luftwaffe on the Eastern Front from almost the first days of the campaign. Despite its *blitzkrieg* reputation, however, the German air forces were not well organized for ground support in the early years of the war. Only small units of dedicated ground attack aircraft using Hs 123 biplanes and Bf 109s modified to serve as fighter bombers were in operation, later joined by Fw 190s modified to serve as fighter bombers and Hs-129 ground attack aircraft. Repeated crises on the Eastern Front, however, led to incessant calls that Bf 110s, Ju 87s, Ju 88s, and even He 111 bombers be used in the ground attack role. The Chief of the Luftwaffe General Staff, General Gunther Korten, created a consolidated Schlachtflieger inspectorate in the fall of 1943 with similar authorities to the existing fighter, bomber, and reconnaissance inspectorates, and ground support organization, tactics, and communication procedures all improved as a result.

The Me 262 was a revolutionary jet aircraft, but problems with engine reliability kept operational numbers low. Soviet fighters only encountered the jets during the last weeks of the war, as most were dedicated to opposing Allied strategic bomber operations. (Bettmann via Getty Images)

The dominant Luftwaffe fighter bomber on the Eastern Front in the last years of the war was the Fw 190. It carried 20mm cannon in addition to machine guns to strafe targets, and could carry 500kg of bombs. The Fw 190s typically sought to attack vulnerable Soviet truck convoys and other soft targets, aiming to stop the Soviet tanks by cutting off their supplies. By 1945, wing-mounted Panzerschreck and Panzerblitz rocket launchers improved the Fw 190's antitank capabilities. The Panzerschreck consisted of the 88mm infantry bazooka-style antitank rocket-launcher mounted in triple or quadruple tubes under the wing. The weapon could penetrate 160mm of armor, but only had a range of 150 meters, making the launching aircraft vulnerable both to ground fire and the explosion generated by a successful hit. The Panzerblitz mounted an 81mm shaped charge warhead on a rocket body, and "garden fence" racks were used to mount 12 on an Fw 190. The Panzerblitz arrangement allowed for firing at longer range. The weapons were effective but in short supply, and even in April 1945 only 12 of 61 fighter bomber squadrons had the Panzerblitz and just two the Panzerschreck.

The Ju 87 Stuka, famed for its precision dive-bombing attacks in the early years of the war, was consolidated under the fighter bomber directorate with the Fw 190 and soldiered on in limited numbers on the Eastern Front into 1945. Dive-bombing attacks had proven costly as the USSR was increasingly able to defend key targets with fast-firing antiaircraft defenses, forcing the use of shallow-dive or low-altitude attacks that reduced vulnerability but were less accurate. By the end of the war, many of the remaining Ju 87s had been transferred to night bomber units. Some Stukas were upgraded in 1943 with two 37mm Flak 18 cannon, and the famous tank-killing ace Hans-Ulrich Rudel used the up-gunned Stuka Ju 87G to great effect. The Hs 129 was one of the few aircraft produced by Germany as a dedicated ground attack aircraft, but its engines proved disappointing and it was never fielded in large numbers. The original 30mm cannon armament was upgraded to 37mm and ultimately 75mm, and in 1944 and 1945 the

Small numbers of Stukas continued to operate with Luftwaffe ground attack units into 1945. The Ju 87G version had two 37mm cannon mounted under the wings, and if used to attack Soviet tanks from the sides or rear could be effective. The famous Stuka tank-killing ace Hans Ulrich-Rudel, who claimed to have knocked out 519 tanks during the war, favored the Ju 97G model. (Nik Cornish at www.Stavka.photos)

A German Hs 129B ground attack aircraft, captured and in US markings after the war. The Hs 129 was designed to serve as a ground attack aircraft, and was originally equipped with a 20mm cannon, later increased to 37mm and 75mm in some versions. Never produced in large numbers, only a few squadrons still flew the Hs 129 in 1945.(USAAF)

remaining Hs 129s were concentrated in a few squadrons. Cannon-equipped aircraft with 37mm or less armament had to approach their tank prey from the sides or rear at low level and close to within 200 yards, making them vulnerable to any antiaircraft assets protecting their targets.

Bombers

Despite the incessant demands for close air support for the beleaguered ground forces, the Luftwaffe's senior leadership continually sought a way for the air force to play a more strategic role in weakening the enemy. A bomber force was built up in 1943 and 1944 with 300 He 111s and numerous of the new but troubled He 177 long-range bombers, and plans developed to strike key Soviet factories as far away as Gorki to the east of Moscow. In the end, the movement of the front westwards forced these plans to be abandoned, and the bombers instead were used in early 1944 against a series of rail junctions in the southern USSR to disrupt the looming Soviet summer offensive. The rail campaign was of limited utility, but the Luftwaffe's bomber force did score a strategic success with a night raid in June 1944 on Poltava that destroyed 47 of the 73 B-17s that had landed in Soviet-held Ukraine on a shuttle bombing mission, leading the Allies to abandon the program.

As 1944 progressed, the Luftwaffe bomber force was steadily drawn down both through attrition and the disbanding of units due to fuel shortages, and partially in the hopes that the V-1 and V-2 bombardments would fulfill its offensive role. Western fighter and antiaircraft defenses were virtually impenetrable, and on the Eastern Front the intense pressure on German ground forces led to a renewed emphasis on fighter defense and fighter bomber operations to support the troops. In January 1945, the Luftwaffe order of battle contained 294 bombers, many used for training or pressed into service to help the remaining Ju 52 transports flying supplies into cut-off German positions. As the launching areas for the V-1 against England had been lost with the defeat in France, KG 53's He 111s were used to launch the flying-bombs against targets in Britain. By April 1945, only 37 multi-engine bombers remained, and these were mostly Mistel (Mistletoe) composite bomber units. The Mistel consisted of an unmanned Ju 88 packed with explosives, flown to the target by a Bf 109 or Fw 190 fighter mounted atop the bomber and released as it dove on the target. Plans had been underway to strike key hydroelectric dams in the USSR with the Mistel force, but once the Soviet offensive began in January 1945 they were used in attacks against bridges over the Vistula and Oder rivers.

Ground crew loading bombs on an He 177 bomber. The He 177 had a troubled development, but the Luftwaffe was able to field a strategic bombing force of 300 He 111s and He 177s. Fuel shortages and the demands of the front led to a focus on fighter and fighter-bomber operations, and the bomber force was largely disbanded by 1945. (Nik Cornish at www.Stavka.photos)

Night operations

The Luftwaffe's night fighter defenses had inflicted heavy losses on RAF bombing operations in early 1944, but by the beginning of the following year had been rendered almost impotent due to the loss of its forward radar early warning line in France and crippling fuel shortages. On the Eastern Front, the Luftwaffe conducted improvised night bomber operations. During the early years of the war over the USSR, the Soviets had used obsolete biplanes for night harassment bombing, some flown by the famous "night witches" female pilots. In the later years of the war, Luftwaffe units began to use a variety of obsolete aircraft, miscellaneous trainers, and captured enemy aircraft to conduct similar night operations over Soviet positions. The aircraft could attack with light bombs and machine-gun fire and were almost impossible for enemy radars to track. Several hundred light night bombers were operating on the Eastern Front by late 1944.

Reconnaissance and transport

Strategic and tactical reconnaissance was a source of Luftwaffe superiority in the early years of the war. Ju 88 bombers began to take over the strategic reconnaissance role in 1943, and with the increasing threat posed by enemy fighters, the Germans began to use Bf 109s and Fw 190s modified to carry cameras for tactical reconnaissance. Typically, two fighters would conduct the sortie, with one flying cover for the photo recon aircraft. As the war progressed, daylight reconnaissance sorties became more and more hazardous, and the Luftwaffe made more use of Do 17Zs using flash-bombs to illuminate the landscape for photo runs. In the West, the Luftwaffe employed about 40 Ar 234 and Me 262 jets for reconnaissance purposes.

The Luftwaffe still primarily relied on the Ju 52 for air transportation in 1945, augmented by small numbers of other aircraft including some He 111s used as transports. The force had

been under enormous pressure throughout the war, suffering major losses in Crete and during attempts to resupply German positions at Stalingrad and in Tunisia. By January 1945, 206 transports remained in the order of battle, shrinking to just ten in April. The Luftwaffe made use of Df 230 gliders to land supplies in encircled fortresses such as Breslau, with light Fieseler Fi 156 Storch aircraft retrieving the pilots for subsequent glider runs. The pressure on the limited number of transports pushed the force to breaking point as it struggled to resupply isolated Axis garrisons in Hitler-designated fortresses in Budapest, Breslau, Konigsberg, and ultimately, Berlin itself.

The Mistel, named for the parasitic mistletoe plant, included a worn-out Ju 88 bomber with the cockpit and nose packed with explosives flown to and released against the target by a manned Bf 109 or Fw 190 fighter. By 1945, the limited number of Mistels were the primary bomber asset operated by the Luftwaffe. (ullstein bild via Getty Images)

Ground support and bases

The Soviet 1945 offensive forced the Luftwaffe to rapidly evacuate its many bases in Poland, with the attendant loss of large amounts of supplies and maintenance equipment. German industry prioritized production of complete aircraft rather than spare parts, so the Luftwaffe often drew on new-production aircraft rather than repairing older ones, and the Soviets found large numbers of non-operational aircraft littering captured airfields. The German training infrastructure had been relocated to Poland to decrease the vulnerability to roving US and British fighters, but was also overrun by the Soviet assault. Once driven into Germany, however, the Luftwaffe was able to use the many sophisticated and relatively well-equipped permanent bases in the Reich to support its last months of resistance.

Flak and ground forces

The Luftwaffe controlled major antiaircraft and ground forces. By late 1944, 1,250,000 personnel – roughly half the strength of the Luftwaffe – manned its seven Flak corps, 29 divisions, 13 brigades, and 160 regiments. Flak units both provided static defense of German cities and other point targets and deployed with the ground forces. Heavy Flak units employed 88mm, 105mm, and 128mm guns, and medium and light units 20mm

The Luftwaffe employed a wide variety of aircraft such as this Bücker Bü 131 Jungmann (young man) trainer to conduct night bombing and harassment operations over Soviet lines later in the war. The practice was begun by units at the front, almost certainly inspired by similar VVS night harassment operations conducted since the first days of the war and adopted by Luftwaffe leadership as a force-wide practice given its effectiveness. (Nik Cornish at www.Stavka.photos)

and 37mm versions. Captured weapons were increasingly incorporated into the force as the war progressed. By the last months of the war, German fighter defenses of the Reich had largely collapsed, and Flak inflicted more losses than the fighter force. As Soviet and Western Allied forces drove into Germany, the Flak batteries were employed in direct fire support to augment the ground forces' defense.

The Luftwaffe also contributed large numbers of personnel directly to the ground battle. In response to a directive to transfer personnel to the army in 1942, Goering countered with a plan to field 22 Luftwaffe field divisions under air force leadership. However, the units performed poorly and by 1945 had largely been shattered, the remnants being integrated into army units. More effective were the Fallschirmjager parachute divisions and the Hermann Goering Panzer Division, expanded into a corps-level formation by the last year of the war. As the defenses of the Reich collapsed in 1945, more and more Luftwaffe ground personnel found themselves swept up into ad hoc ground defense units for the final stand.

Senior commanders

The Luftwaffe suffered from systemic weakness at the high command level. Reichsmarschall Hermann Goering was, among many other offices and formal responsibilities, the commander-in-chief of the Luftwaffe. A World War I ace with 22 kills, Goering led the famous Jagdgeschwader Richthofen and was an early member of the Nazi Party. He was named commander of the Luftwaffe at its unveiling in 1935, and was at the height of his power and popularity during the first triumphant years of the war. As the Luftwaffe struggled to defend against the Allied bomber offensive and defeats multiplied on every front,

The Luftwaffe controlled most of the Third Reich's Flak assets, and its excellent 88mm anti-aircraft gun had proven an excellent antitank weapon from the war's early days. By 1945, Flak units would be heavily engaged as Soviet and Western Allied units began to overrun German territory. (audiovis.nac.gov.pl/obraz/Wikimedia Commons)

his standing declined sharply. Never attentive to his Luftwaffe command responsibilities, Goering withdrew further as the situation deteriorated and by 1945 only attended command conferences with Hitler when summoned. The position of Luftwaffe Chief of the General Staff (OKL) had proven troubled during the war, with General Hans Jeschonnek committing suicide in August 1943, and his successor, General Guenther Korten, dying of wounds received during the bomb plot against Hitler in July 1944. General Werner Kreipe replaced Korten, but after a heated session with the Fuhrer concerning the Luftwaffe's failings was banned from any further attendance at the Fuhrer conferences, leaving no senior Luftwaffe representation at the table until General Karl Koller was appointed to the position two months later.

The major Luftwaffe formation on the Eastern Front in 1945 was Luftflotte 6, commanded by General and later Field Marshal Robert Ritter von Greim. Greim was a 28-victory ace from World War I who became an enthusiastic supporter of Hitler and the Nazi Party in the early postwar years. Greim aided Chiang Kai-Shek in establishing an air force in China from 1924–27, rose rapidly in the new Luftwaffe during the late 1930s, and led the V Fliegerkorps in France in 1940. In June 1941, Greim began four years of almost uninterrupted combat leadership on the Eastern Front. After initially operating with Army Group South, Greim was placed in charge of Luftwaffe Command East in April 1942 to support Army Group Center's defensive operations. His airmen provided excellent support despite the diversion of most Luftwaffe resources to Stalingrad. In July 1943, Greim's command was upgraded and designated Luftflotte 6. Greim combined extensive Eastern Front experience with fanatical loyalty to the Nazi cause, and Hitler regarded him as a potential replacement for the indolent Goering.

General Martin Fiebig served under Greim during the last months of the conflict as an air corps commander. A World War I bomber pilot, Fiebig had the remarkable experience of leading a group of seven officers in the 1920s to serve as instructors and advisors to the VVS at various schools in the Moscow area as part of the covert German–Soviet military

Ju 87 Stuka dive-bombers in action over Narva in April 1944. The venerable Stuka served into 1945 on the Eastern Front, with a number dedicated to night bomber duties. (ullstein bild via Getty Images)

cooperation program of the era. During the war, Fiebig led the bombers of KG 4, then took over the VIII Fliegerkorps in 1942. Given charge of the Stalingrad airlift, Fiebig made all possible efforts to supply the encircled 6th Army despite his warnings that the task was impossible. After service in the Balkans, Fiebig returned in 1945 to command the II Fleigerkorps under Greim, redesignated Luftwaffenkommando Nordost on April 12.

The other major commander in the East during 1945 was General Otto Dessloch, the commander of Luftflotte 4. Dessloch served in the Imperial Air Service during World War I as both a pilot and observer, and afterwards with the right-wing Freikorps in Bavaria. He went to the USSR from 1926–27 to attend the secret German–Soviet fighter pilot school in Lipetsk. He served in the West and then with Luftwaffe units on the Eastern Front, and assumed command of Luftflotte 4 in June 1943 from Field Marshal Wolfram Freiherr von Richthoften. Dessloch was briefly ordered to the West to take over the shattered Luftflotte 3 in the summer of 1944, but soon returned to his Luftflotte 4 Eastern Front command. In the last days of the war, Dessloch took command of the collapsing Luftwaffe elements fighting the final Allied offensives when Greim was elevated to command of the Luftwaffe.

Order of battle

Structure

The basic Luftwaffe unit was the squadron (*Staffel*), initially consisting of ten aircraft and ten pilots for single-engine aircraft and 40 aircrew for multi-engine aircraft. A few vehicles and 80–150 ground staff provided support. Squadron strength could be changed for special purposes – for example, in 1944, efforts were made to expand fighter squadrons to 16 aircraft – and was increasingly impacted in 1945 by serviceability, fuel shortages, and losses as the Allies closed in. Air groups (*Gruppen*), the rough equivalent of the VVS regiment, consisted of three squadrons; three Gruppen made up an air wing (*Geschwader*), similar

General Robert Ritter von Greim. Von Greim had fought almost continuously on the Eastern Front since 1941 and was regarded by Hitler as one of his hard-fighting commanders. Greim commanded Luftflotte 6 until the last days of the war, when Hitler called him to the Fuhrerbunker, promoted him to marshal and gave him command of the Luftwaffe. Greim was the second and last commander of the Luftwaffe, if only for a few days, and the last officer Hitler promoted to marshal rank. (ullstein bild Dtl. via Getty Images)

in size to a VVS division. The Luftflotte was the major, all-arms command formation and provided dedicated support to a Wehrmacht army group. Various formations, including Kommands, Luftkorps, and Fliegerdivisions, were used to provide an intermediate level of control between the Luftflotte and Geschwader levels or to independently control aviation assets covering sections of the front.

In January 1945, the Luftwaffe fielded seven Luftflotte headquarters, although these varied greatly in strength. To the west, Luftflotte 3 had been given additional aircraft and fuel reserves to support the Ardennes offensive and contained 1,304 aircraft, including 101 bombers and 196 ground attack aircraft, but Luftflotte 5 in Norway only operated 342,

Fw 190 and Stuka ground support aircraft. Given the need to support the ground forces, the majority of Schlachtflieger ground support *Schlachgeschwader* (SGs) served on the Eastern Front during the last several years of the war. As the Soviets stormed across Poland, the Luftwaffe stripped the Reich of fighter units, many specialized for engagements with strategic bombers, and threw them into intense combat over the Oder River. (Nik Cornish at www.Stavka.photos)

and Luftflotte 2 in northern Italy a mere 50 aircraft. Luftflotte Reich had a total of 1,245 aircraft, including 254 day fighters and 723 night fighters, to defend the homeland against Allied bomber offensives and fighter sweeps. Luftflotte 1, with 215 aircraft, supported Army Group North's 20-plus divisions cut off on the Courland Peninsula. German defenses in East Prussia and along the Vistula River line in Poland were supported by Luftflotte 6 with 822 aircraft. This force contained the highest number of fighter bombers of any Luftwaffe formation, 278. Luftflotte 4 supported German forces to the south on the Eastern Front with 588 aircraft, including 199 fighter bombers.

Luftwaffe Order of Battle, January 1945

Luftflotte 6

Day fighter units: JG 51, JG 52 (Bf 109)
Night fighter units: NJG 5, NJG 100 (Bf 109, Ju 88)
Bomber unit: KG 55 (Ju 88, Ju 188, Do 217)
Ground attack units: SG 1, SG 3, SG 77 (Ju 87, Fw 190)
Night ground attack units: NSGr 126 (Go 145, Ar 66, Hs 126, Fiat CR 42, Ju 87)
Maritime Reconnaissance unit: SAGr 126 (Ar 196, Bv 138)
Strategic Reconnaissance units: FAGr 1, 3 (Ju 188, Me 410) and AGr 22, Nacht, 122 (Ju 88, Me 410, Ju 188, Do 217)
Tactical Reconnaissance units: NAGr 2, 3, 4, 8, 15 (Bf 109, Fw 190)
Transport Unit: TG 3 (Ju 52)

Luftwaffe Order of Battle, April 1945

Luftflotte 6

Day fighter units: JG 1, 3, 6, 11, 77 (Bf 109, Fw 190)
Bomber units: KG 4, 53 (He 111)
Ground attack units: SG 1, 2, 3, 4, 9, 77, 151 (Fw 190, Ju 87)
Night ground attack units: NSGr 4, 5, 8 (Ju 87, Si 204, Ar 66, Go 145)
Strategic Reconnaissance units: FAGr 2, 3, 100, 121, 122, AGR 11, 22, Nach Aufkl (Ju 88, Ju 188, Me 410, Do 217, Si 204)
Tactical Reconnaissance units: NAGr 2, 3, 4, 8, 11, 13, 15, 31, Panzer recon units (Bf 109, Fw 189, Bf 110, Si 204)
Maritime Reconnaissance units: SAGr 126, BFGr (Ar 196, Bv 138)

CAMPAIGN OBJECTIVES

The road to Berlin

The Red Army's 1945 offensive into Germany was designed to utterly destroy German power and secure Soviet domination of Central Europe. Stalin was determined that his forces take Berlin to crown the USSR's costly victory over Nazi Germany and remained convinced that the Western Allies would try to seize it before Soviet troops. In January 1945, the Red Army's two most powerful fronts – the 1st Belarussian and 1st Ukrainian – were marshaled under Stalin's most capable leaders, Zhukov and Konev, and ordered to smash through the thin German defenses of Army Group A, transit the Polish plain, and cross the Oder. Stavka planners considered a follow-on attack on Berlin possible as early as February.

Il-2M Shturmoviks over a snow-covered landscape. Advancing the start date of the Vistula–Oder and East Prussia offensives from late January to the 12th–14th in response to Churchill's request meant the attack began during a period of sustained poor weather, forcing the cancellation of large numbers of the VVS's pre-planned attack sorties. (Nik Cornish at www.Stavka.photos)

Despite his fixation on Hitler's capital, Stalin and the Stavka high command were diverted from their primary goal after reaching the Oder in early February. The Soviet offensives in 1945 were launched on a broad front across Eastern Europe, with Red Army forces attacking to clear East Prussia and take Konigsberg to the north of Zhukov's and Konev's offensive, while other fronts to the south were to capture besieged Budapest and drive into Austria. Additional forces assisted Tito's Yugoslav forces. After the rapid dash across Poland, Zhukov and Konev were halted on the Oder River by logistical problems and poor weather. Despite Berlin lying only 60–70km from the lead Soviet bridgeheads over the Oder in early February, the final assault would be delayed until mid-April as Konev and Zhukov secured their flanks in Silesia and Pomerania. Political factors also played a role as Stalin, with a watchful eye on geostrategic developments, noted that the postwar status of Austria had not been clarified at the Yalta Conference, and ordered offensives by his forces south of the Carpathian Mountains to complete the conquest of Hungary and advance on Vienna and Prague, potentially expanding the postwar Soviet sphere.

Operationally, although Stalin was more than willing to pay the cost in blood to raise the Red Banner over the Reichstag, Soviet forces in 1945 strove to minimize casualties. The early years of the war had cost millions of dead and wounded, and manpower was

The big three sit for a portrait at the Yalta Conference, February 4–10, 1945. General Antonov of the General Staff, directly behind Stalin, began the conference by briefing the success of the Vistula–Oder operation, but it soon became clear that Zhukov's offensive had been halted on the Oder River and Stalin ordered attacks to secure its flanks. (US Government public domain)

becoming limited, even for the USSR. Red Army ranks were augmented by freed prisoners and civilians from liberated regions of the Soviet Union during 1944, but most Soviet rifle divisions advancing through Poland and into Germany remained understrength. As a result, the Red Army strove to replace flesh with steel, using firepower and integrated action by artillery, tanks, and aircraft to break through German defenses rather than costly frontal assaults by infantry.

In Berlin, any coherent plans for victory were increasingly replaced with demands that the Wehrmacht and the German people prevail through sheer will and dedication to the Nazi cause; and failing that, resist to the end. With the failure of the Ardennes offensive, Hitler could no longer postulate a coherent path to survival, but instead retreated to an emphasis on his iron will, endurance at the front, and vague hopes for something akin to the collapse of the alliance against Prussia that saved Frederick the Great from defeat in 1762. Operationally, Hitler continued to retain forces in Norway and Courland, and send scarce military resources to secondary theaters, leaving the front in Poland undermanned in January 1945. Only when the Red Army reached the Oder River in February did he allow a buildup to defend Berlin. Almost to the last day, Hitler issued orders to weakened and sometimes nonexistent units to attack and relieve

Berlin. Throughout, he continued to demand bitter resistance to the end, and viewed the destruction of Germany's people and infrastructure as the direct result of their lack of sufficient Nazi ardor to fulfill his vision.

The last year of the war saw the Luftwaffe desperately pursue a variety of strategies to gain some sort of advantage over its foes. By the beginning of 1945, it was clear that many of the new weapons were either not having a decisive effect – such as the V-1 and V-2 missiles and the Me 262 – or were still unready for fielding. Fighter leaders including Adolf Galland urged that a mass attack by 2,000 interceptors could inflict such heavy losses on an Allied raid, perhaps 400 bombers or more, that at least a temporary halt in the strategic bombing offensive would follow, but the available fuel and fighter reserves were expended to little effect in the Ardennes offensive and Operation *Bodenplatte*. Another approach was to use ramming operations to bring down Allied bombers. Using lightened Bf 109s that would be able to outclimb defending Allied fighters, the German aircraft would then plunge down and ram the bombers, with the pilots having at least some chance to bail out. Although a mass attack was envisaged, just 250 aircraft and pilots were ready in Sonderkommando Elbe and thrown into combat when Allied advances on the ground threatened to overrun Germany in March, and only a small number of bombers were downed. Luftwaffe plans remained ambitious to the end; as late as March 26, Luftwaffe Chief of Staff Karl Koller briefed Hitler on Operation *Eisenhammer* (Iron Hammer), a plan to use 82 Mistel composite bomber-fighter combinations against steam and hydroelectric power stations in the Moscow region. The attack would be launched at night from East Prussia, with Ju 88s and Ju 188s along with Ju 90s and Ju 290s serving as pathfinders to mark the route and illuminate the targets with flares, and the strike aircraft would recover at bases in the isolated Courland Peninsula pocket. The crews were actually preparing to take off for the attack when weather delayed the mission, followed by orders to redirect the Mistels against the Oder bridges.

The Soviet officers who led the assault into Central Europe and Germany, pictured in 1945. Konev, on the left, and Zhukov, in the lighter uniform in the center, led the 1st Ukrainian and 1st Belarussian Fronts from Warsaw into Germany. General Chernyakovsky (not pictured) led the 3rd Belarussian Front in East Prussia, but was mortally wounded in February 1945 and Marshal Vasilevsky, third from left, assumed command. Marshal Rokossovsky, fourth from the right, led the 2nd Belarussian Front throughout 1945. (Victor Temin/Hulton Archive via Getty Images)

THE CAMPAIGN

Air war over Poland and Germany

By 1945, the VVS had perfected ground–air coordination techniques, with Air Force liaison teams embedded with advancing armored units to call in air support as needed. The advance of Konev's and Zhukov's tank armies across Poland in January 1945 was covered by rotating formations of Shturmoviks and fighters to reconnoiter, cover flanks, and strike any centers of resistance. (Courtesy of the Central Museum of the Armed Forces, Moscow via www.Stavka.photos)

January 1945: The Vistula–Oder Offensive

Despite Hitler's assertion to Guderian, the Red Army's buildup on the Vistula was anything but a bluff. Zhukov's 1st Belarussian Front and Konev's 1st Ukrainian Front severely outnumbered the German defenders both on the ground and in the air, with a total of 2,250,000 troops, 6,500 tanks and self-propelled guns, over 32,000 guns and mortars, and almost 5,000 combat aircraft. The two fronts alone contained almost one-third of all Soviet infantry formations and over 40 percent of the armor on the entire Eastern Front, and the two air armies in support more than a third of VVS combat aircraft. General Sergey Rudenko's 16th Air Army and General Stepan Krasovsky's 2nd Air Army were attached to Zhukov and Konev, respectively. The 3rd Fighter and 9th Ground Attack Corps, 183rd Bomber, 242nd Night Bomber, and 1st Guards Fighter Divisions had been dispatched from the Stavka reserve to strengthen Rudenko's air army with over 1,000 additional combat aircraft for the offensive.

The Wehrmacht faced this buildup on the Vistula with 400,000 troops, 1,150 tanks and assault guns, 4,100 artillery and mortar tubes, and less than 1,000 aircraft. Of 18 panzer divisions on the Eastern Front, only five were on the Vistula, and Hitler insisted that the two panzer reserve corps be placed closely behind the thinly held front line. General von Greim's Luftflotte 6 controlled 882 combat aircraft, with less than 300 supporting Army Group A in Poland facing Zhukov and Konev, and the remainder supporting Army Group Center in East Prussia. Fuel shortages and poor weather reduced Greim's reconnaissance efforts, and the 1st Belarussian Front reported only 112 enemy flyovers in early January. The Luftwaffe had a strong Flak force available, however, with a total of 200 batteries with 900 guns in Poland and East Prussia.

Despite the poor weather conditions in November and December, the 2nd and 16th Air Armies flew over 3,500 reconnaissance sorties and photographed 109,200km^2 of the attack zone, with particular attention to potential river crossing sites along the planned lines of advance. VVS fighter regiments used their radar network to keep enemy aircraft from penetrating an 80–100km exclusion zone concealing the buildup. For *maskirovka* purposes, the Soviets camouflaged their bases, and built 818 mockups of aircraft at 55 dummy airfields to confuse German intelligence as to the main axis of attack. The decoy airfields were attacked 19 times during the day and five times at night, while the camouflaged main airfields remained unhit.

Shturmovik ground attack and fighter divisions or corps were attached to each attacking army for direct support, while bomber units and additional fighter divisions were kept under Rudenko's and Krasovsky's control to be employed where needed. Detailed strike plans were drawn up for targets to be hit in the first four days of the offensive. The 16th Air Army planned 13,374 sorties, 7,945 during the first two days, and the 2nd Air Army 12,080 and 8,650, respectively. Soviet fighters were almost completely dedicated to covering the Shturmoviks and light bombers, and the 2nd Air Army only planned 249 sorties against Luftwaffe airfields – 2 percent of the total. Once Konev's and Zhukov's four tank armies were inserted into the battle, the Il-2M and fighter units would shift to directly support the breakthrough and exploitation. Engineer-airfield and airfield service battalions were ready to move forward with the tank armies to rapidly establish new airfields for VVS operations.

Soviet aircraft flying over a heavily shelled front line. In January 1945, Zhukov's and Konev's massive artillery barrages alone shattered German defenses despite the poor flying weather that hindered initial air support from the VVS, but in East Prussia Chernyakovsky's artillery failed to allow a breakthrough on the first day of his offensive. (Courtesy of the Central Museum of the Armed Forces, Moscow via www.Stavka.photos)

Combat Aircraft, Vistula–Oder Offensive, 1945

Air army	Total aircraft	Fighters	Assault	Bombers	Night bombers	Recon/Spotters
16th VA	1,275	637	300	192	83	63
Reinforcements for 16th VA	1,015	361	395	137	91	31
Total 16th VA	2,290	998	695	329	174	94
2nd VA	2,582	1,172	775	417	114	104
Total	4,872	2,170	1,470	746	288	198

The Soviet airmen trained intensely for the offensive. On December 20, the 2nd VA rehearsed an air attack on a full mock-up of German defenses, with simulated targets including tanks, artillery positions, bunkers, and Flak nests. As the exercise began, fighters of the 5th and 6th Fighter Corps made low-level strafing attacks to neutralize antiaircraft defenses, followed by a formation of level bombers dropping heavy ordnance to destroy target bunkers. Pe-2s of the 2nd Guards Bomber Corps led by General Ivan Polbin launched a series

OPPOSITE VISTULA–ODER AND EAST PRUSSIAN OFFENSIVES, JANUARY 1945

of precision dive-bombing attacks followed by 1st Guards Ground Attack Corps Shturmoviks flying attack runs on the tanks and trenches. The Il-2Ms followed the Pe-2s so rapidly they encountered dust raised by bomb impacts. General K. V. Kraynyukov reported that even the Luftwaffe in its glory days could not achieve such a concentrated use of air power.

Stalin's pledge to Churchill to advance the offensive's start date forced Konev and Zhukov to attack during several days of heavy snow and fog. Konev's 1st Ukrainian Front nevertheless began the assault on January 12, relying on a heavy artillery barrage shelling enemy positions up to 16km deep. Despite the fog, Krasovsky ordered his Po-2 spotter planes aloft to fly under the clouds and identify surviving German positions for the second barrage. Po-2s caught sight of the main German reserve force, the XXIV Panzer Corps, on the move and artillery was shifted to hit the advancing panzers. Small numbers of Il-2Ms with experienced crews were able to fly in pairs over the assault waves of infantry and T-34s and JS-2 tanks. Some clearing during the afternoon allowed Krasovsky to order additional sorties, and the 2nd Air Army airmen flew a total of 468 on the 12th, about 10 percent of those planned, with 271 of these hitting ground targets and 87 being for reconnaissance. In response to desperate pleas for air support, Greim sent 63 reconnaissance and 57 fighter bomber sorties aloft, while 47 German fighters tried to strafe the attackers, but Luftwaffe pilots claimed only a single tank and three VVS aircraft destroyed. The assault elements had torn a hole 70km wide in the German front and Konev was able to commit his second echelon force, the 3rd Guards and 4th Tank Armies. By nightfall, the forward elements had pushed 20km deep. On day two of the offensive, Krasovsky was able to increase his operations tempo to 698 sorties, 124 for reconnaissance and 339 to bomb and strafe the retreating XXIV Panzer Corps. The 4th Bomber and 2nd Ground Attack Corps struck the road-bound panzer columns with waves of nine to 12 aircraft. The 2nd Air Army also dedicated some of its fighters to free hunting patrols and blockades over Luftwaffe airfields, with any German aircraft attempting to get into the air facing immediate interception by orbiting Kobra, Yak, or Lavochkin fighters. The German defensive line on the Vistula was shattered, with the survivors desperately trying to withdraw to the west.

General S. I. Rudenko commanded the 16th Air Army during 1945. The 16th contained the largest number of aircraft of any air army employed during World War II during the Berlin operation – 3,188. (Unknown/Wikimedia Commons)

Zhukov's 1st Belarussian Front began its offensive on January 14. An hour before the initial artillery barrage, Rudenko was able to launch an attack on the headquarters of the reserve LVI Panzer Corps using his most experienced night bomber crews. The poor flying conditions during the morning forced Rudenko to cancel most of the planned air attacks, however, and the 16th Air Army only flew 33 daylight sorties on the 14th. Despite the lack of VVS support, Zhukov's first barrage was so effective that he called off the second, and the 1st and 2nd Guards Tank Armies drove rapidly through gaps in the German lines. Air operations intensified over both Konev's and Zhukov's fronts on the 15th despite continuing poor weather, with the VVS hitting any retreating German columns spotted through the fog and destroying bridges along likely lines of retreat. Rudenko's

1. January 12–16: despite poor flying weather, Marshal Zhukov's 1st Belarussian and Marshal Konev's 1st Ukrainian Fronts shatter German defenses.
2. January 13–16: the offensives by Marshal Rokossovsky's 2nd and General Chernyakovsky's 3rd Belarussian Fronts initially bog down, but good flying weather on the 16th allows for the 4th and 1st Air Armies to help the fronts' second echelon forces break through.
3. January 17: Warsaw falls to the 1st Polish Army.
4. Zhukov's 1st Belarussian front seizes Lodz and besieges Posen; many Luftwaffe airfields are overrun.
5. January 20: concerned with the 3rd Belarussian Front's slow start against East Prussia, the Soviet High command orders Rokossovsky's 2nd Belarussian Front to change its axis of advance to the north to cut off German forces around Konigsberg, even though Chernyakovsky has begun to make progress.
6. Konev's troops are directed to seize the Silesian industrial zone.
7. Zhukov reaches the Oder River.
8. 150km separate Zhukov's and Rokossovsky's forces.
9. February 15–21: German Army Group "Vistula" Launches Operation *Sonnenwenda* against Zhukov's flank.
Front Line, January 12, 1945
Front Line, January 31, 1945
Baltic Sea
POMERANIA
EAST PRUSSIA
POLAND
SILESIA
Konigsberg
Danzig
Suwalki
Kustrin
Frankfurt
Posen
Warsaw
Lodz
Breslau
Krakow
Oder
Warte
Vistula
Elbe
XXXXX Vistula HIMMLER
XXXXX Center
XXXXX 3 Belarussian CHERNYAKOVSKY
XXXX 18 GOLOVANOV
XXXX 1 KHRYUKIN
XXXX 4 VERSHININ
XXXXX 2 Belarussian ROKOSSOVSKY
XXXX 6
XXXXX A
XXXXX 1 Belarussian ZHUKOV
XXXX 16 RUDENKO
XXXX 6
XXXXX Center SCHORNER
XXXXX 1 Ukrainian KONEV
XXXX 2 KRASOVSKY
N
0 100 miles
0 100km

A Luftwaffe Bf 109 fighter flying low in the cloudy conditions typical of air combat in 1945. Greim struggled to respond to desperate calls for help from Army Group A when the Soviet offensive began, hindered both by weather and his lack of aircraft. (Nik Cornish at www.Stavka.photos)

Luftwaffe General von Greim with his staff on the Eastern Front in late 1943. Von Greim had fought on the Eastern Front with only brief interruption since the start of Operation *Barbarossa*, giving him extensive experience in battling the VVS. Greim made every effort to hit Zhukov's and Konev's forces in January 1945, but to little effect. (Roger Viollet via Getty Images)

airmen flew 181 sorties, 102 against enemy ground forces, and Krasvosky's airmen 510. The Luftwaffe mounted 244 missions on January 15 and its 132 fighter bomber sorties reported the destruction of 13 of Konev's tanks, while JG 52 Bf 109s claimed to down 10 VVS aircraft for the loss of two of their own.

Although Hitler designated Warsaw a fortress – as he would numerous other cities in the East in 1945 – it was only defended by four fortress battalions and some engineer detachments. Zhukov's 47th Army attacked to the north of the city on January 15, and despite the blizzards rapidly broke through, threatening the city with encirclement. The 1st Polish Army led the attack into the ruins, supported by almost 1,000 sorties flown by the Polish 4th Mixed Air Division. Warsaw fell on January 17 after four days of assault. The loss of a major capital triggered a hysterical response from Hitler, who again denounced his generals for withdrawing without orders. The commanders of both Army Group A and the 9th Army were summarily relieved and the OKH Chief of Operations arrested and sent to a concentration camp.

January 16 brought clear flying weather at last, and both Soviet and German airmen took to the sky in strength. Greim's Luftflotte 6 launched 414 fighter bomber and 173 support sorties. SG 77 reported success with rocket attacks on the advancing Soviet armored columns with their Panzerschrek-equipped Fw 190 F-8s, although it lost seven aircraft to enemy action during the day. The 16th Air Army at last could surge its operations, and flew 3,431 sorties, 1,481 by Il-2Ms, and claimed to down 18 German aircraft in 24 separate air engagements. Rudenko's and Krasovsky's Shturmoviks repeatedly struck retreating Wehrmacht armor, their primary target, with regimental-sized strikes. Like all World War II airmen, Soviet pilots made exaggerated claims, and the 300th Ground Attack Division reported destroying 3,500 vehicles. The advancing 65th Tank Brigade, however, came upon 12 burned-out tanks, 120 destroyed vehicles, and 200 enemy bodies on the road between Radom and Tomaszow, confirming the effectiveness of the 9th Ground Attack Corps' Shturmovik attacks hours before. A series of precision Pe-2 dive-bombing attacks on a bridge west of Warsaw stalled a column of several thousand vehicles evacuating Warsaw that were repeatedly attacked by Krasovsky's Il-2Ms and Pe-2s, claiming 500 destroyed.

Air engagements on January 16 underscored how the balance in the air had shifted from the early years of the war, when Luftwaffe *Experten* shot down huge numbers of VVS "foals" – novice pilots – flying inferior aircraft. Now, VVS fighters used the *Experten*'s tactics, downing German aircraft with repeated high-speed diving gun passes against the Luftwaffe fighter bombers. In a typical action, six La-5s and Yak-9s escorting ten Shturmoviks over Warsaw spotted a formation of SG 1 Fw 190 fighter bombers and immediately attacked, forcing the Focke Wulfs to jettison their bombs. In the ensuing dogfight, the VVS pilots shot down four of the Fws with no losses, including squadron leader and Knight's Cross holder Major Otto Hulsch in his Fw 190 F-8 "White One." The Luftwaffe recorded the loss of 18 aircraft on January 16 and 32 on the 19th, and JG 52 alone suffered the loss of 17 Bf 109s between the 17th and 18th. Rudenko and Krasovsky dominated their opponents, flying a total of 11,748 total sorties from January 12–17 in support of the breakthrough, while Greim's Luftwaffe pilots only managed 2,184.

January 1945: The East Prussia Offensive

To the north, the 3rd Belarussian Front under General I. D. Chernyakovsky began its attack on January 13 directly into East Prussia. The 2nd Belarussian Front under Marshal K. K. Rokossovsky attacked a day later to his south to protect the northern flank of Zhukov's drive across Poland. The fronts had a combined strength of 1,670,000 troops, 28,360 heavy guns and mortars, 3,300 tanks and self-propelled guns, and were supported by over 3,000 VVS combat aircraft. Khryukin's 1st Air Army, with 1,333 serviceable combat aircraft, was attached to Chernyakovsky, and Vershinin's 4th Air Army, with another 1,647, to Rokossovsky. Marshal Golovanov's long-range bomber force, now organized as the 18th Air Army, was assigned to lend its firepower to the offensive. Unlike the thinly spread German defenses in Poland, however, Army Group Center was well positioned to put up a stout resistance. The Wehrmacht had 580,000 troops and 700 tanks and self-propelled guns defending a shorter front, and was able to exploit East Prussia's more defensible terrain and prewar defensive works. Greim had stationed more of his Luftflotte 6 aircraft here – 500 fighters and fighter bombers, 90 bombers, and 90 reconnaissance aircraft than in Poland, but the German airmen were still outnumbered by a six-to-one margin.

Khryukin and Vershinin planned thoroughly for the operation. *Maskirovka* featured heavily in Khryukin's preparations, and he constructed dummy airfields with 100 ground attack and 60 fighter mockups in the Suwalki area, complete with radio traffic to simulate operations by an air army staff, ground attack corps, and three bomber divisions, to convince the Germans that would be the primary axis of attack. Khryukin planned 2,575 sorties on the first day and 2,335 on the second, with 80 percent supporting the main

1st Air Army commander Khryukin. Khryukin had a varied prewar career, serving during the Spanish Civil War and being sent to China to command a squadron of Tupelov SB-2 bombers in China. During the war, Khryukin organized the defense of the vital Murmansk railroad in 1941 and led the 8th Air Army during the decisive Stalingrad campaign before taking over the 1st Air Army. (Unknown/Wikimedia Commons)

breakthrough by the 5th Army. The 130th Fighter Division was tasked to strafe enemy reserves while the 303rd patrolled the battlefield and attacked German airfields. By the fourth day, support would shift to the planned exploitation by the 11th Guards Army and 1st Guards Tank Corps, the front's second echelon. The 1st Air Army's two bomber divisions were held directly under Khryukin's control to strike enemy rail links and be available to support any sector as needed.

The East Prussian operation						
Air armies	Total aircraft	Fighters	Assault	Bombers	Night bombers	Recon/Spotters
1st VA	1,333	536	453	212	86	46
4th VA	1,647	680	634	181	122	30
Totals	2,980	1,216	1,087	393	208	76

To the south, Vershinin's 4th Air Army planned to deliver 2,817 tons of bombs during the first three days, with 10,033 sorties. Unlike the 1st Air Army, the 4th Air Army planned to use more of its combat power to strike deeper behind the German front line. A-20 Havoc bombers of the 5th Bomber Corps would strike the German 2nd Army and Army Group Center headquarters, as well as railroad yards and depots. The 325th Night Bomber Division's Po-2 light bombers would hit artillery positions and the XX Army Corps HQ. On the day of the attack, the 196th, 199th, 233rd, and 260th Shturmovik divisions would support the planned main breakthrough by the 2nd Shock Army and 48th Army, with 840 sorties planned to strike German positions with waves of 44–57 Il-2Ms continuously for five hours.

Although Golovanov's bombers successfully executed a 740-bomber raid on German defenses the night before the offensive, the same thick fog and low cloud conditions that frustrated air operations on the Vistula forced Khyrukin to cancel the planned initial 1st Air Army massed strike by 545 bombers and Il-2Ms. Worse, the impact of Chernyakovsky's 120,000-shell artillery barrage was limited as the German forward defenses were left lightly manned and the Soviet assault troops took heavy losses trying to penetrate the main line of

A crewman in front of his Il-4 bomber. Golovanov's 18th Air Army's long-range bomber force was allocated to supporting the offensive into East Prussia in January 1945. (Courtesy of the Central Museum of the Armed Forces, Moscow via www.Stavka.photos)

A Shturmovik under camouflage netting. The 1st Air Army launched a major *maskirovka* effort to convince German intelligence that the main thrust of the 3rd Belarussian Front's attack would be on the Suwaki axis. The main effort was actually to be launched further north. (Courtesy of the Central Museum of the Armed Forces, Moscow via www.Stavka.photos)

resistance. Luftflotte 6 units made a strong effort to support the front in East Prussia despite the weather, flying 140 sorties, primarily Fw 190 fighter bombers, losing eight along with four other aircraft. On January 14, the weather cleared around 1400hrs and the 1st Air Army was able to carry out 490 sorties – 257 of these being Il-2Ms – claiming the destruction of 40 counterattacking tanks and 80 motor vehicles, plus the suppression of 12 artillery batteries. The Luftwaffe flew 250 sorties, and groups of 25–60 German fighter bombers repeatedly bombed and rocketed the bogged-down Soviet infantry and tank assault units. VVS fighters claimed to down 25 enemy aircraft, but after two days of costly fighting none of Chernyakovsky's armies had achieved a clear breakthrough.

The 4th Air Army's aircraft were grounded by the poor weather when Rokossovsky launched his offensive on January 14, and only managed 40 sorties the next day, most of them for reconnaissance. Like the 3rd Belarussian Front to its north, the 2nd Belarussian Front made only slow progress against strong German defenses for several days, but the front-wide good flying weather on the 16th proved decisive for both stalled fronts. Vershinin's airmen were able to fly 2,500 sorties and deliver 1,800 tons of bombs to support the 5th Guards Tank Army's decisive breakthrough, allowing the second-echelon 5th Guards Tank Army to move forward. By the 19th, a 100km gap had been forced in the German front line and lead units had advanced up to 60km, heavily supported by VVS fighters and Shturmoviks. The Luftwaffe tried to slow the onslaught by massing its Fw 190 fighter bombers, but Soviet fighters intervened. Major Ivan Borisov and Captain Pavel Golovachyov of the elite La-7-equipped 9th Guards Fighter Regiment – known as the regiment of the aces – shot down two Fw 190s apiece. SG 3 reported the loss of five Fw 190s during the action, while JG 51 lost six Bf 109s. Golovachyov brought his score to 26 several days later when he downed four of the five Fw 190s claimed by 9th Guards pilots intercepting a formation of 25 Focke Wulfs.

The good flying weather on January 16 also enabled the 3rd Belarussian Front to finally break through. Although the planned 5th Army main effort remained bogged down, Chernyakovsky shifted the 1st Guards Tank Corps and 11th Guards Army to its north to exploit an unexpected weakening of the defense in another attack zone. Three hundred and forty-two 1st Air Army bombers were rapidly sent to hit German positions and prepare the way, followed by 284 strikes against enemy defensive positions further back. The breakthrough force was ultimately supported by a fighter division, five bomber, and three Shturmovik divisions. As the tanks and infantry drove forward, air liaison officers in the leading units called in 1st Guards Ground Attack Corps Il-2s to strike any strongpoints holding up the assault, while Shturmoviks of the 182nd Guards Division prowled the right flank for targets and the 277th Guards Assault Division the left. The 130th Fighter Division flew air cover over the entire operation. The Luftwaffe's desperate attempts to halt the breakthrough by attacks with groups of 50 fighters and fighter bombers were repeatedly bounced by VVS fighters. Air support from the 1st and 4th Air Armies had been critical to Chernyakovsky's and Rokossovsky's breakthroughs on the 16th, the air armies flying a combined total of 2,800 sorties.

The exploitation

By January 17, Konev and Zhukov had torn a hole 500km wide in the Vistula defenses, and Chernyakovsky and Rokossovsky had broken through German defenses in East Prussia. In Poland, Soviet mechanized forces were advancing 30–70km a day, with VVS fighters and Il-2Ms overhead covering the tank armies. Konev seized Krakow on January 18 and Zhukov's 8th Guards Army – led by General Vasily Chuikov, the hero of Stalingrad – took Lodz on the 19th after pausing to fire green flares to warn off VVS aircraft that mistook his column for a German one. Luftflotte 6 launched a maximum effort on the same day, flying 813 sorties and hitting the Soviet tank armies with groups of 20–50 fighter bombers. German airmen reported the destruction of 40 tanks, 178 motor vehicles, and 36 aircraft, but were nevertheless unable to slow the Red Army advance. The Soviets responded with 1,900 sorties and claimed 32 enemy aircraft destroyed. Throwing fighter bombers against well-covered Soviet columns was costly; SG 77 began the battle with 101 operational Fw 190s and 16 Stukas, but lost about a quarter of the force between January 20 and 22 alone. Attrition also cost the Luftwaffe some of its valuable *Experte* veterans, with seven Luftwaffe holders of the Knight's Cross – the Third Reich's highest decoration – killed in action during the month. In East Prussia, the sustained attacks by Fw 190 fighter bombers on the 3rd Belarussian Front goaded Khryukin to launch a series of attacks against German airfields around Konigsberg, and the 1st and 277th Guards Assault Division and 6th Guards Bomber Division reported 65 Luftwaffe aircraft destroyed on the ground and 40 damaged. In an unusual action on January 20, a group of Shturmoviks from the 4th Air Army's 90th Guards Ground Attack Regiment led by Captain Lyadsky encountered a group of Hs 129s, their Luftwaffe counterpart aircraft, and were able to shoot down three.

Marshal Rokossovsky, on the left, speaking with Zhukov. Both marshals were infuriated by the January 20 order from the high command changing Rokossovsky's 2nd Belarussian Front's axis of advance from the northwest to the north. The attack cut off German forces in East Prussia, but opened a 150km gap between his forces and Zhukov's 1st Belarussian Front. (Sovfoto/Universal Images Group Editorial via Getty Images)

The Red Army advance captured more than 130 Luftwaffe airfields in Poland, most littered with non-operational aircraft and abandoned supplies and equipment. On January 22, SG 9 had to scramble its fighter bombers as Soviet tanks approached its base west of Posen. Twenty Hs 129s and Fw 190s were abandoned on the field, and another eight Fw 190s were lost attacking the tank column from the air. The Soviet advanced guards claimed upwards of 700 mostly non-operational German aircraft were abandoned on the large network of airfields around Posen, a claim so high that the skeptical commander of the 1st Guards Tank Army appointed a survey commission to confirm it. On occasion, the VVS arrived as former occupants, bypassed by the Soviet tank columns, were scrambling to depart. The 402nd Fighter Regiment began to land at Sochaczew Airfield west of Warsaw only to take fire from German troops still holding positions on the perimeter of the base. The Germans attempted to make abandoned airfields unusable, and shortages of auto transport and traffic congestion hindered the VVS airfield engineer battalions as they tried to move forward and establish new airbases. On January 18, most Soviet aircraft were still operating from their original bases east of the Vistula, and only elements of the 6th Guards Fighter Corps and 1st Guards Ground Attack Corps had successfully moved to new airfields north of Krakow. By January 24, the 16th VA's bases were still 150–200km behind the lead ground forces, and the 2nd VA's airfields 100–150km behind.

As the pursuit gained momentum, the Soviet high command issued revised orders to the advancing fronts. On January 20, the Stavka ordered Rokossovsky to shift his attack axis north to cut off German forces in Prussia due to concerns with Chernyakovsky's slow advance, even though the 3rd Belarussian Front had by this point begun to break through. The orders enraged Rokossovsky and Zhukov, as they peeled support away from the 1st Belarussian Front as it raced towards the Oder River and Berlin. Zhukov was directed to continue through Posen towards the Oder and Berlin despite his weakened flank protection. On Zhukov's left, Konev was ordered southwest to take Breslau and seize Upper Silesia, the last intact industrial area left to the Reich. The Soviets swept into the area from the north, driving the German defenders out rather than encircling them to minimize battle damage to the 100-plus Silesian coal mines and numerous steel- and synthetic oil-producing plants. The loss of the area reduced Fw 190 production capacity by 25 percent and overran the V-1 test site near Katowice, complete with intact missiles.

The halt on the Oder

At the Yalta Conference in early February, General Antonov of the General Staff briefed Roosevelt, Churchill, and Stalin that Soviet forces had inflicted 400,000 casualties on the Germans and destroyed an estimated 45 divisions. In 18 days, the front had moved almost 500km from the vicinity of Warsaw to the Oder, less than 100km from Berlin. Zhukov's and Konev's artillery and tanks had played the key role in breaking the thin German lines on the Vistula due to the initial poor flying weather, but as conditions improved, Rudenko and Krasovsky had been able to increase operations. The 16th and 2nd Air Armies flew a total of 25,400 sorties and downed 209 enemy aircraft in 214 aerial engagements in January. VVS losses were low, only 343 from all causes, reflecting the rapid collapse of resistance on the Vistula and Greim's inability to maintain sorties as Luftflotte 6's bases were overrun. The Soviet offensive cost the Luftwaffe the aircraft assembly and repair plants and the *Fliegerschule* network of training airfields that had been established in Poland to escape Allied strategic bombing raids. On February 1, elements of the 1st Belarussian Front established small bridgeheads over the Oder and Zhukov submitted plans to the Stavka to renew the assault on Hitler's capital after a brief pause.

Despite the success of the Soviet January offensive, the final march on Berlin would be delayed for months. A heavy storm of mixed snow and rain brought all operations to

An Fw 190 squadron in late 1944. In response to the Soviet offensive across Poland, the Luftwaffe stripped the Western Front and defenses of the Reich to reinforce the Oder River line. Numerous German airmen trained and equipped for high-altitude engagements with US strategic bombers found themselves suddenly thrust into low-level strafing runs on Soviet units trying to establish bridgeheads over the river. (ullstein bild Dtl. via Getty Images)

a halt, followed by warming temperatures that thawed the ice on the Oder and hindered crossing operations, while also turning Polish roads and the VVS's forward field airstrips into quagmires. Damage to the rail network forced the Red Army to rely on trucks to bring up supplies, but the thaw brought resupply operations over the muddy roads to a virtual halt. In addition to logistical difficulties, Stalin and his high command were now concerned with Zhukov's flanks, particularly the 150km gap opened by their January 20 decision to divert Rokossovsky north towards the Baltic coast. The need to besiege Posen and other lesser bypassed fortresses further weakened the 1st Belarussian Front's strength on the Oder. A sharp deterioration in Red Army discipline posed additional problems. Fired by pre-offensive indoctrination of the troops by political officers (commissars) calling for vengeance, many Soviet troops engaged in a campaign of plunder, rape, and murder when they reached German territory. Soviet commanders resorted to harsh measures to restore a measure of unit cohesion and order in the ranks.

As Zhukov's troops clung to shallow bridgeheads over the Oder, the aircraft overhead now carried black crosses rather than red stars as the Luftwaffe gained local air superiority for the last time. Like the logistics convoys, VVS airfield engineer and support battalions had to struggle forward on roads made impassible by the sudden thaw. Worse, what field airstrips had been established were turned into morasses and the VVS began to lose more aircraft to landing and take-off accidents than enemy action. Imaginative leaders turned to using the autobahn for improvised runways, a measure already used by the Luftwaffe. Colonel A. I. Pokryshkin's 9th Guards Fighter Division first experimented with the concept of using highways as airstrips, followed by Lieutenant Colonel L. I. Goreglyad's 22nd Guards Fighter Division. Pokryshkin was careful to camouflage his P-39 Kobras alongside the roadway, and the Luftwaffe had to conduct a series of low-level reconnaissance runs to find the base. When the Germans were finally able to launch raids against the Kobras, they still had difficulty destroying the dispersed and hidden aircraft.

While most of the VVS bases were unusable, the Luftwaffe was now able to operate from its permanent network of airbases in German territory, complete with hangers and concrete runways. The collapse of the Vistula front had also galvanized the Luftwaffe high command to hastily dispatch all available fighting strength to the East. Six fighter air wings – JGs 1,

3, 5, 6, 11, and 77, amounting to 650 fighters – were stripped from the air defenses of the Reich. SG 4 was taken from the Ardennes front, bringing an additional 100 Fw 190 fighter bombers to the Oder. Greim received command of all operational and training units on February 1 and control of Berlin's Luftwaffe defense force two days later. All 445 day and night fighters were stripped from the capital and ordered to serve in the ground attack role against the Soviet crossings. With the arrival of reinforcements, Greim's Luftflotte 6 had roughly 1,300 combat aircraft available on the Oder in early February, 750 of them day fighters. Only half were operational, but priority was now on the defense of Berlin, and the German high command ordered all available fuel reserves sent to Greim. The Wehrmacht OKW war diary noted at the time that "air operations on all other war theaters are in comparison of absolutely negligible importance."

Most of the fighter units transferred were trained and organized to engage Allied strategic bombers and were unprepared for low-level strafing and bombing missions. One air group of JG 4 was equipped with the heavily armored Sturmbach version of the Fw 190 and had been successful against US heavy bomber formations, but lost nine aircraft in its first day of combat on the Eastern Front and six the next. Even Captain Eric Hartman, the Luftwaffe's leading ace with over 300 victories, had trouble preparing his new command for the harsh realities of combat in the East when assigned to lead a newly transferred JG 53 air group. Greim's numbers began to tell, however, and in addition to bombing and strafing Zhukov's bridgeheads over the Oder, the Luftwaffe struck the thousands of Soviet supply trucks mired in the mud or jamming the few hard-surface roads leading to the front, reporting the destruction of 51 tanks and almost 2,000 trucks during the first three days of the month. The Luftwaffe flew a record 1,403 sorties on January 27, claiming to destroy eight Soviet tanks, 20 artillery pieces, 30 vehicles, and eight aircraft at the cost of 30 German aircraft. The next day, weather reduced the Luftwaffe to 608 sorties, but they claimed to destroy a further 14 tanks, 40 guns, and over 800 Soviet vehicles. Soviet observation posts reported spotting 13,950 enemy overflights during the first ten days of February, while, crippled by the impact of the thaw, Rudenko's 16th VA could only get 624 aircraft into the air during the same period.

On February 2, General Vasiliy Chuikov was able to get advanced elements of his 8th Guards Army across the Oder despite the weakening ice, along with a few antiaircraft guns mounted on skis. The next day, however, he had to halt all daylight operations due to continuous bombing and strafing by waves of Fw 190s. On Chuikov's northern flank, the 5th Shock Army reported 5,008 individual attacks by Luftwaffe aircraft on February 2 and 3. German aircraft also raided the few VVS forward airfields, on February 4 killing Major

Soviet machine guns on an antiaircraft mount. Soviet forces desperately struggled to protect their tenuous bridgeheads over the Oder against incessant Luftwaffe bombing and strafing runs in early February. Chuikov's 8th Guards Army was able to move some heavy AAA over the frozen river on sleds before the sudden thaw began to melt the ice. (Nik Cornish at www.Stavka.photos)

An Il-2M on a grass airfield. The VVS struggled to establish new airfields hundreds of kilometers from the offensive's start line, with many of the abandoned German facilities rendered inoperable. Soviet aircraft were briefly able to operate from primitive field strips, but these were turned into quagmires by the early February thaw. (Courtesy of the Central Museum of the Armed Forces, Moscow via www.Stavka.photos)

Sergey Kiselyov of the 3rd Fighter Corps staff, an 18-victory ace who had been in combat since 1941. To the south, Konev's forces seized crossings over the Oder River to the north and south of Breslau, but the Luftwaffe mounted continuous attacks to pin them in their bridgeheads. Luftflotte 6's VIII Fliegerkorps controlled operations in the area and threw all available aircraft, including Bf 109 fighter units, into repeated low-level attacks. The German airmen managed 280 sorties against the bridgeheads on January 24, repeatedly bombing and strafing the crossing sites but taking losses to Soviet fighters and antiaircraft fire. Luftflotte 6 reported good success with the Panzerblitz rockets mounted on its fighter bombers. Air Group I of SG 2 claimed 74 tanks during February, and Air Group III of SG 4 reported 23 destroyed by its Fw 190s between January 21 and March 16.

German troops to defend the river had been thin on the ground, but the Luftwaffe attacks gave time for reinforcements to arrive. An ad hoc grouping of Volkssturm militia and Hitler Youth drove out a Soviet force that had taken the city of Kustrin on the east bank of the river, and German forces retained another major bridgehead to the south at Frankfurt-an-der-Oder. On Konev's front, the surviving elements of the XXIV Panzer Korps, informally known as "Nehrings roving cauldron," regained German lines after their escape from the Vistula and were immediately returned to the front to help stabilize the line. The Fuhrer ordered the creation of a new Army Group Vistula to control forces gathering on the Oder and in Pomerania to the north, and to the dismay of OKH Chief of Staff Heinz Guderian and senior army leaders, Reichsfuhrer-SS Heinrich Himmler was given command. Himmler lacked any experience in military matters and rarely left his command train, but by early February he was leading an army group that included over 30 divisions. The high command also rushed 300 antiaircraft guns that had been defending German cities to the Oder, where their high-velocity shells proved lethal to Soviet tanks.

The Luftwaffe had played a major role in stabilizing the front in the East, arguably prolonging the war by several months. However, the cost was high, with 107 aircraft lost while flying 3,300 sorties from January 31 to February 2. In early February, Stuka ace

The VVS first began to use autobahns as improvised airstrips during the February thaw, that rendered its field strips unusable. The Luftwaffe also used the autobahns for the same purpose, with Ju 88s hidden in the trees in this photo next to the road. (EN Archive)

Colonel Hans-Ulrich Rudel, commander of SG 2, was hit while flying his Ju 87G against Soviet forces near Breslau. After destroying 12 Soviet tanks, Rudel's aircraft was struck by antiaircraft fire as he set a 13th on fire. Rudel was able to land, but his wounded leg had to be amputated. Attrition and fuel shortages soon began to reduce the Luftwaffe's ability to generate sorties. Greim's Luftflotte 6 flew 7,300 sorties per week during the first part of February, but that number fell to 2,900 per week for the first two weeks of March. The VVS began to regain its strength over the front line as its basing and logistical support improved, and on February 12 the German OKW war diary noted 1,133 Luftwaffe sorties and 1,500 by the Soviets. Loss rates began to favor the VVS fighters as they repeatedly bounced German fighter bomber formations. The Luftwaffe reported the loss of 25 aircraft while claiming 12 victories on February 13, and the destruction of 21 for only five kills the next day. On February 20, stung by these losses, Greim ordered a force-wide shift to free hunting fighter sweeps all along the front. The Soviets were taken by surprise with the sudden change and lost 54 aircraft on the first day and another 20 on the second, at a cost of just 11 and seven German aircraft, respectively. The Soviets suffered particularly high losses of Il-2s, but the diversion of German aircraft from the ground attack role eased the pressure on Red Army ground forces.

Hans-Ulrich Rudel attacks Soviet tanks over the Oder, February 9, 1945

During early February, the Luftwaffe temporarily gained air superiority on the Oder River front and threw all available aircraft into battle to try and halt Soviet river crossing operations. On February 9, 1945, the famous Stuka ace Hans-Ulrich Rudel and his unit scrambled in response to reports of Soviet tanks just north of Frankfurt-an-der-Oder. Rudel began a series of attack runs on a column of 13 T-34s and JS-2s, eventually setting 12 ablaze. Soviet antiaircraft units in the area didn't use tracers and their positions were only revealed by flashes when firing. Due to the inexperience of the other Stuka pilots, Rudel ordered them to orbit the area and try to suppress the Soviet AA when identified. The scene shows Rudel's final attack on the remaining JS-2 tanks. Rudel was able to set them on fire with his last 37mm round, but a Soviet AAA round hit his Stuka, smashing his right foot. Rudel was able to land successfully, but his right leg had to be amputated below the knee. Rudel returned to the air in late March, and, an unrepentant Nazi and Hitler supporter, escaped to Argentina after the war.

Jim Laurier

OPPOSITE CLEARING THE FLANKS AND SEIZURE OF KONIGSBERG

The turn to the flanks – February–March 1945

As Zhukov struggled to maintain his bridgeheads on the Oder line in early February, Stalin and his high command began to revise their plans. Zhukov and Konev needed a pause to restore the rail network and build up supplies, and the VVS required time to establish a usable forward airfield network. On the Oder, Zhukov was ordered to eliminate the remaining German bridgeheads and strengthen his own. Stalin remained concerned by the vulnerability of Zhukov's flanks, perhaps haunted by the memory of the 1922 Polish counterattack that drove the Red Army from the gates of Warsaw. The Soviet fronts were now ordered to attack south into Silesia and north to eliminate what was dubbed "The Pomeranian balcony." Geopolitical factors also likely played a major role in Stalin's calculations. He continued to fear that the Allies might try to race to Berlin before the Red Army, but in February Soviet forces were less than 100km from the city while the Western Allies were still bogged down in difficult fighting west of the Rhine. The Yalta Conference in early February had allocated Berlin to the Soviet occupation zone in Germany, but the delineation of postwar zones in Austria had not been settled. Stalin judged he would have sufficient time to expand the Soviet postwar sphere of influence in the south before seizing Berlin.

On February 8, Konev's 1st Ukrainian Front launched attacks from his bridgeheads over the Oder to the north and south of Breslau. The ability of Krakovsky's 2nd Air Army to operate was still limited by poor weather and problems with basing, and it only averaged 546 sorties per day from February 8–14. Konev's progress on the ground was nevertheless initially rapid, with the 3rd Guards and 4th Tank Armies advancing 60km on the first day of the offensive. The Luftwaffe's Fliegerkorps VIII launched vigorous attacks to try to halt the Soviet tank columns, losing 19 aircraft on the first day of the offensive and 43 on the second. The VVS suffered a notable loss when one of its most famous airmen, General Major Ivan Polbin – who had pioneered Pe-2 dive-bombing tactics and was the commander of the 6th Bomber Corps – was killed when his aircraft took a direct hit from Flak on February 11. The Luftwaffe attacks helped German forces slow Konev's advance, and his spearheads ultimately reached but halted on the Neisse River. The 5th Guards and 6th Armies met on

Ju 52 transports flying over a German civilian refugee cart in 1945. As the Soviets attacked south into Silesia and north into Pomerania, the small remaining Luftwaffe Ju 52 force struggled to fly supplies into surrounded fortresses such as Breslau and cut off units in Courland and East Prussia. Attempts to evacuate civilians placed additional pressure on Germany's limited air, sea, and ground transportation resources. (Nigel Dobinson/SSPL via Getty Images)

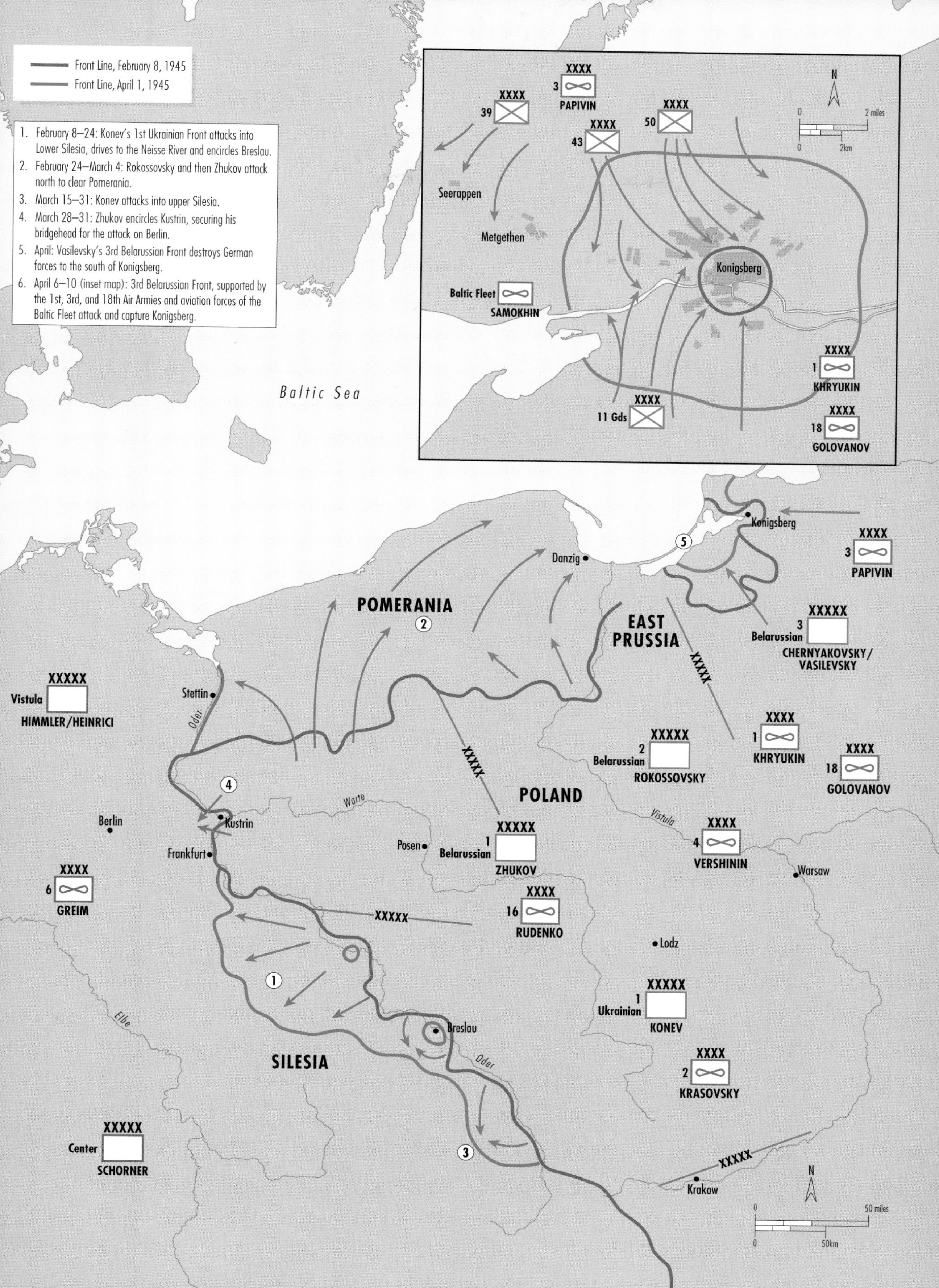
Front Line, February 8, 1945
Front Line, April 1, 1945
1. February 8–24: Konev's 1st Ukrainian Front attacks into Lower Silesia, drives to the Neisse River and encircles Breslau.
2. February 24–March 4: Rokossovsky and then Zhukov attack north to clear Pomerania.
3. March 15–31: Konev attacks into upper Silesia.
4. March 28–31: Zhukov encircles Kustrin, securing his bridgehead for the attack on Berlin.
5. April: Vasilevsky's 3rd Belarussian Front destroys German forces to the south of Konigsberg.
6. April 6–10 (inset map): 3rd Belarussian Front, supported by the 1st, 3rd, and 18th Air Armies and aviation forces of the Baltic Fleet attack and capture Konigsberg.
Baltic Sea
XXXX 3 PAPIVIN
XXXX 39
XXXX 43
XXXX 50
Seerappen
Metgethen
Konigsberg
Baltic Fleet SAMOKHIN
XXXX 1 KHRYUKIN
XXXX 11 Gds
XXXX 18 GOLOVANOV
N
0 2 miles
0 2km
Konigsberg
Danzig
POMERANIA
EAST PRUSSIA
XXXXX 3 Belarussian CHERNYAKOVSKY/VASILEVSKY
XXXXX Vistula HIMMLER/HEINRICI
Stettin
Oder
XXXXX 2 Belarussian ROKOSSOVSKY
POLAND
Warte
Berlin
Kustrin
Frankfurt
Posen
XXXXX 1 Belarussian ZHUKOV
Vistula
XXXX 4 VERSHININ
Warsaw
XXXX 6 GREIM
XXXX 16 RUDENKO
Lodz
Elbe
XXXXX 1 Ukrainian KONEV
Breslau
SILESIA
Oder
XXXX 2 KRASOVSKY
XXXXX Center SCHORNER
Krakow
N
0 50 miles
0 50km

One of the more unusual German aircraft that operated, although only briefly, on the Eastern Front was the Focke-Achgelis Fa 223 helicopter. Only 20 were produced, and five Fa 223s were at Templehof airport in Berlin when one was ordered to Danzig amidst the Soviet offensive in late February. After an arduous flight, it arrived in Danzig on 5 March only to discover the city was under attack and escaped along the Baltic coast. The pictured Fa 233 is one of the captured models and is marked with a US white star. (EN Archive)

February 15 and encircled Breslau, another city designated a fortress by the Fuhrer, trapping 35,000 German troops.

Hitler demanded that Luftflotte 6 supply Breslau by air, and Greim turned to General Friedrich-Wilhelm Morzik, the Luftwaffe's expert on air supply operations. Only roughly 100 transports were available, and Morzik was concerned that an operation to supply Breslau would cripple his ability to deliver the 160 tons of supplies the isolated forces on the Courland Peninsula needed daily. Reinforced by some squadrons from Hungary, the Luftwaffe nevertheless attempted to sustain the city, with Greim dedicating a quarter of his fuel supply to the transports in late February. As at Stalingrad, He 111 bombers were used to augment the airlift. Soviet radar-directed fighter defenses forced the supply planes to fly mostly at night, but still inflicted a 10 percent sortie loss rate. Desperate, the Luftwaffe turned to air-dropping supplies from night bomber biplanes and Bf 109s. Red Army advances took the last airfields in the city on April 7, restricting the Luftwaffe to airdrops, DF 230 gliders, and light liaison aircraft. The last run was by seven gliders on May 1, with the pilots retrieved by two Storch light aircraft from an improvised road strip. In total, the last large-scale Luftwaffe airlift operation delivered 1,800 tons of supplies between February 15 and May 1 at the cost of over 165 transport aircraft.

In March, the Stavka determined that Konev's left flank required additional security, and the 4th Tank Army – now designated a Guards unit – was shifted 180km further east from its position on the Neisse River, 120km from Berlin, to lead an attack by the 1st Ukrainian Front's left-wing armies. Krasovsky's 2nd Air Army had 1,737 combat aircraft available in support and placed an emphasis on attacks against German airfields. Poor morning weather grounded Krasovsky's airmen during the first hours of the operation, and only 1,283 of 2,995 planned sorties were flown. The next day, the 2nd Air Army flew 1,697 missions, 750 of these against enemy troops directly on the front line. VVS strikes on German counterattacking forces were effective; in a typical action, the 34th Guards Rifle Corps reported a German counterattack by a battalion supported by ten tanks and the aviation liaison group at corps headquarters called in four Shturmoviks and five fighters in response. Soviet infantry marked targets with rockets and artillery smoke rounds, and the VVS aircraft flew low-level attack runs that scattered the attackers. Soviet pincers met and encircled a German pocket near Oppeln and the 2nd Air Army directed 1,743 sorties to destroy the trapped enemy on March 19 and 20. By the end of the operation, Konev's forces claimed to have destroyed around 40,000 enemy troops and captured 14,000 more, although the 4th Guards Tank Army and 2nd Air Army faced a long redeployment west when Stalin ordered his forces to mass against Berlin in early April.

To the north, the threat posed by German forces in Pomerania was underscored by an improvised German offensive in February against Zhukov's extended right flank. Guderian had initially proposed an ambitious two-pronged attack that would encircle and destroy Zhukov's forces on the Oder front, but Hitler balked at stripping the necessary forces from the Balkans, Courland, Italy, and Norway. Instead, miscellaneous units were designated the 11th SS Panzer Army and sent into the attack on February 15 from Pomerania, supported by elements of Luftflotte 6. The offensive was named Operation *Sonnenwende* (Solstice) and initial progress alarmed the Soviets, but their antitank guns and tanks brought the attack to a halt in a matter of days. On February 24, Rokossovsky's 2nd Belarussian Front began its own offensive to clear Pomerania, reaching the Baltic coast on March 2. Vershinin's 4th Air Army supported the attack with 1,647 combat aircraft, now operating from more established bases. On March 1, Zhukov's 1st Belarussian Front, supported by sorties from Rudenko's 16th Air Army, joined the offensive north with three armies, including both the 1st and 2nd Guards Tank Armies. Fighting in the air was intense. The Luftwaffe's determination to support its ground forces was exemplified by Lieutenant Walter Brandt of JG 3, who on March 3 destroyed three enemy tanks and 20 trucks, as well as shooting down three Soviet aircraft to bring his score to 42 before being himself shot down. Zhukov's troops reached the Baltic the next day and then pivoted west to secure the line of the northern Oder, while Rokossovsky's forces began to drive east to take Danzig.

As the Soviet offensive isolated pockets of resistance on the Baltic coast, the Kriegsmarine organized a massive sealift, Operation *Hannibal*, to evacuate troops and refugees. The Soviet high command ordered the Baltic Fleet to interdict enemy operations with its air and naval forces. Although the Germans used their surviving major surface combatants in the Baltic for fire support and to aide in the evacuation, the Soviets rarely sent their larger naval units out of the Gulf of Finland and instead relied on mines, submarines, and air operations. Several small combat ships and transports were sunk by Baltic Fleet airmen, but submarines inflicted much greater damage, particularly the loss of between 8,000 and 9,000 soldiers and refugees when the S-13 sank the transport *Wilhelm Gustloff* on January 31. The SMS *Schlesien*, a veteran pre-World War I battleship, became a focus for Baltic Fleet air attack in April. During that month, the *Schlesien* evacuated 1,000 wounded soldiers to Swinemunde at the mouth of the Oder north of Stettin, where the vessel used its four 11in guns to bombard Soviet ground forces. The Baltic Fleet sent relays of aircraft into the attack, including A-20s of

Aircraft ammunition preparation. By late February, VVS airfield engineer and airfield maintenance battalions began to establish a number of better-equipped airfields, allowing improved air support to Zhukov's and Konev's Fronts after the rapid drive across Poland. (Nik Cornish at www.Stavka.photos)

VVS maintenance personnel repairing battle damage on an Il-2M Shturmovik. On the other side of the front, the late-war surge in German fighter production left the Luftwaffe with many more planes than it had fuel or pilots to operate, and ground support staff would often simply replace any aircraft with damage or maintenance issues with a new plane rather than repair it. (Courtesy of the Central Museum of the Armed Forces, Moscow via www.Stavka.photos)

the fleet's 51st Mine-Torpedo Attack Regiment and Il-2 Shturmoviks of the 7th Guards Ground Attack Regiment, escorted by 12th and 21st Fighter Regiment Yak-9s. The *Schlesien* hit a British air-dropped mine while maneuvering and was towed back to Swinemunde and scuttled so its antiaircraft guns could still help defend the port. A strike on May 4 by 16 Il-2s and five A-20s, escorted by 18 Yak-9s, destroyed the ship, either via FAB-1000 bombs or torpedo hits. In total, the Baltic Fleet's air and submarine forces had sunk 161 merchant and naval vessels and 25,000 soldiers and refugees were lost. Despite the lack of Luftwaffe air cover, most of the transports made their transits safely, and the operation ultimately succeeded in evacuating a million troops and 1.5 million civilian refugees.

The fight for the Oder: March–April 1945

During March and April, German and Soviet forces waged a sustained air and ground battle for control of the Oder and Neisse crossings. Hitler demanded that the German bridgehead at Kustrin be held at all costs as it blocked the main highway and road link to the capital. The Luftwaffe, facing increasing fuel shortages, ordered operations in the West confined to jet aircraft from March 4, with all other resources focused on the Eastern Front. On March 9, Luftflotte 6 launched 1,718 combat sorties, its highest number in a month, and shot down 19 Soviet aircraft, but the 16th Air Army was able to respond with 5,300 sorties on March 11, claiming 56 aerial victories.

Month	16th Air Army sorties	Recorded Luftwaffe sorties
February	11,349	17,775
March	25,276	4,330
April	40,673	6,422

On March 18, Guderian succeeded in having Himmler replaced as Army Group Vistula commander by General Gotthard Heinrici, an acknowledged Eastern Front defense expert.

Heinrici inherited a chaotic situation, as Zhukov's 5th Shock Army and 8th Guards Army struck from their bridgeheads north and south of Kustrin, isolating the German garrison four days later. The action generated intense air combat, with the Luftwaffe claiming 26 VVS aircraft shot down on March 22, while the Soviets reported a total of 110 German aircraft destroyed in 117 aerial engagements that day and the next. Hitler insisted on an attack from the Frankfurt bridgehead to strike north and relieve Kustrin. The day after its failure, following a furious exchange, the Fuhrer placed Guderian on convalescent leave, replacing him as OKH Chief of Staff with General Hans Krebs. On March 28, Soviet forces seized Kustrin, digging out the last defenders three days later, and the direct route to Berlin was at last in Zhukov's hands.

Hitler demanded that the Luftwaffe destroy the Soviet-held bridges over the Oder and Neisse to prevent a buildup for a renewed offensive. The effort was entrusted to Colonel Joachim Helbig, commander of LG 1, a demonstration air wing that still retained Ju 88 and Ju 188 bombers, and Colonel Werner Baumbach, the commander of KG 200, the Luftwaffe's special operations unit. Baumbach disposed of a variety of unique weapons, including Hs 239 radio-controlled bombs and Mistel composite bombers. Luftflotte 6 would also throw Fw 190 fighter bombers and Stukas against the bridges. Luftwaffe Chief of Staff General Karl Koller listed the top Luftwaffe priorities for March as destroying all Soviet-held bridges over the Oder and Neisse, as well as using its transports to fly supplies to Breslau and other isolated fortresses.

The Mistels consisted of worn-out unmanned Ju 88s packed with 1,700kg of explosives – in some models arranged as a shaped charge resembling a giant Panzerfaust-syle warhead and called the "elephant's trunk" – carried to the target, aimed, and released by a Bf 109 or Fw 190 mounted on struts above the bomber. Mistels had been initially employed against the Normandy beachhead in 1944, but with little success. Goering's intense desire for a

This is a Ju 88–Fw 190 Mistel composite bomber captured after the war and returned the United States for analysis. The bomber was heavy, difficult to take off, and vulnerable to enemy action. Only a few hits were reported during the Luftwaffe's campaign to destroy Soviet-held bridges over the Oder. (US Air Force/Wikimedia Comons)

Mistel attacks on the bridges at Steinau and Kustrin, March 31 and April 16, 1945

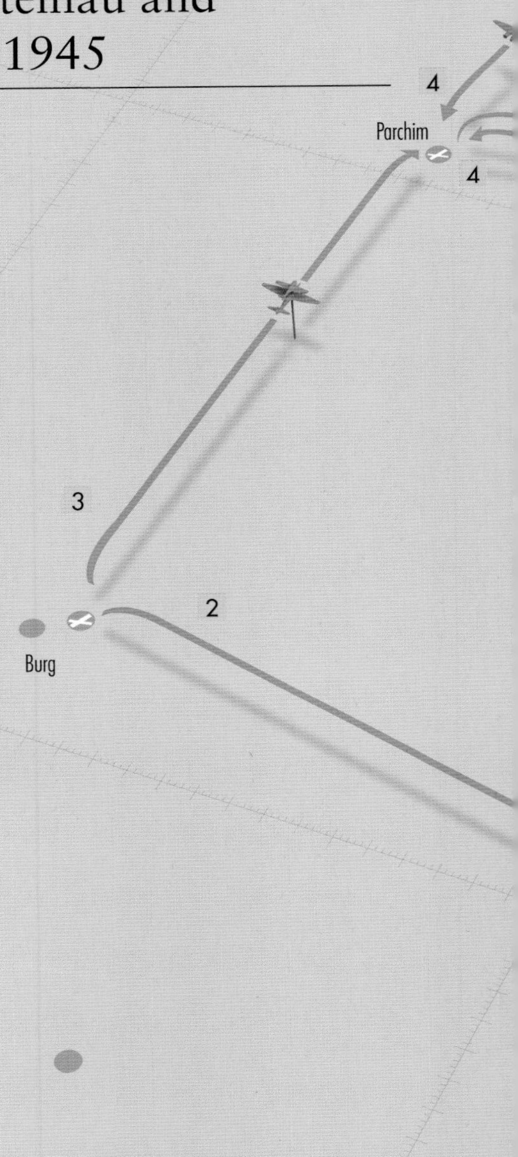

EVENTS

1. March 1945: Hitler orders attacks on the key bridges that can supply a Soviet offensive over the Oder and Neisse Rivers. Colonel Joachim Helbig, commander of LG 1, one of the last Luftwaffe units equipped with bombers, forms an attack unit, using the Mistel composite bombers of KG 200.
2. March 31: After several failed attacks, six Mistels take off from Burg supported by two Ju 88s and two Ju 188s, and are joined by 24 Bf 109s of JG 52 to serve as escort. Three of the Mistels fail to reach the target due to mechanical failures, but three deliver an attack, gliding from 2,500m to 200m through light clouds and Soviet antiaircraft fire. Despite a Soviet smokescreen, there is serious damage to the western end of the rail bridge.
3. April 16: The Luftwaffe launches its second and final successful attack with Mistels. Four Mistels from 6./KG 200 take off from Burg and fly to Parchim airfield.
4. Four Zielfinder (*pathfinder*) support Ju 188s arrive at Parchim from Rostok and Neubrandenburg. One is damaged on landing.
5. The strike package begins to take off around 1700hrs, despite a US bomber and fighter formation overhead. One Mistel is shot down by a Spitfire IX of 411 RCAF.
6. The force assembles near Neubrandenburg for the run-in to the target.
7. The Ju 188s attack Soviet antiaircraft defenses with fragmentation bombs, but one Mistel is shot down during the attack. At least one Mistel achieves a hit, destroying the bridge.

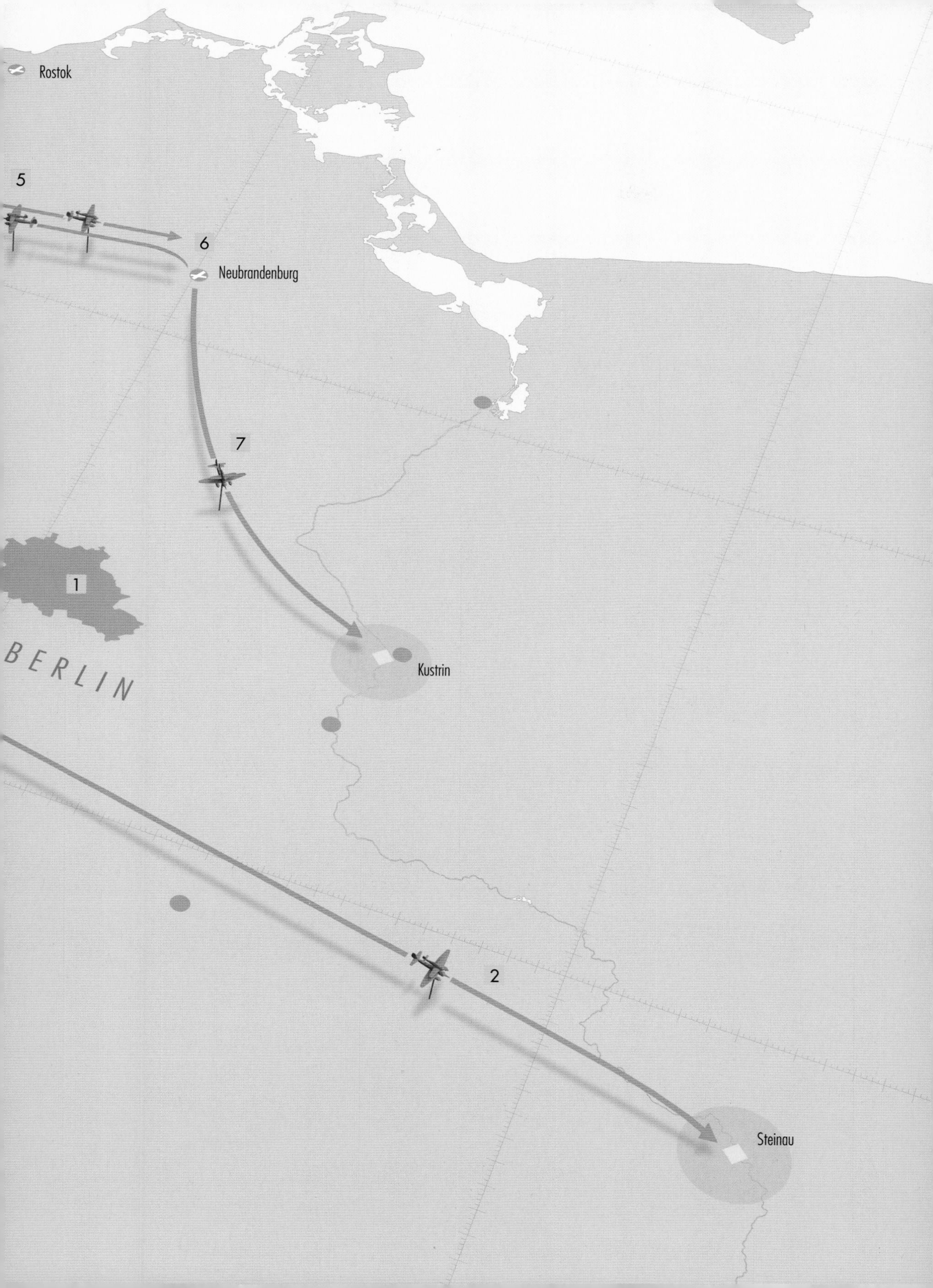

Rostok
5
6
Neubrandenburg
7
1
BERLIN
Kustrin
2
Steinau

high-visibility success led to preparations to use them against the Royal Navy at Scapa Flow; however, the sinking of the *Tirpitz* by bombers allowed the British to dispatch the fleet away from the base for other missions. Planning was underway in early 1945 to use Mistels for Operation *Eisenhammer* (Iron Hammer), raids against Soviet hydro-electric plants in the Moscow region, but they were shifted to the Oder and Neisse target set. The Luftwaffe had almost completely disbanded its bomber force by early 1945, and Helbig and Baumbach controlled its last true long-range strike force. As its peak, the force consisted of 78 bombers and 29 Mistels and would ultimately fly 550 sorties, 200 of them by bombers, against the bridges.

The German effort was initially dispersed against a variety of targets. A series of attacks in early March were launched against the bridges supporting the Soviet bridgeheads over the Oder north and south of Kustrin. A force of 33 SG 3 Fw 190 fighter bombers successfully destroyed one of the Soviet pontoon bridges south of Kustrin on March 1, but four He 111 bombers failed to destroy any of the bridges at the same site despite the use of Hs 239 radar-controlled bombers on March 6. The eight escorting Bf 109s of JG 4 shot down two Yak-9s while protecting the He 111s. Nineteen JG 11 Fw 190s escorted nine SG 151 Stukas to attack the Soviet bridges north of Frankfurt the next day, but again no hits were made. At the end of the month, Mistels scored one of their major successes by severely damaging the rail bridge at Steinau, near Breslau. In this attack, six KG 200 Mistels were supported by two Ju 88s and two Ju 188s to serve as pathfinders and attack Soviet antiaircraft positions, with 24 Bf 109s escorting the strike group. The Mistels suffered from reliability issues and three malfunctioned on the flight, but three others delivered their weapons against the bridge, sliding down to attack from 1,500 meters to just 200 meters through the clouds and light Flak. Air reconnaissance confirmed serious damage to the western end of the bridge.

With the fall of Kustrin to the Soviets on March 31, most of the attack sorties became focused against the large railway and highway bridges there that were soon repaired by Red Army engineers. Soviet defenses became more sophisticated during March, with 235 fighters, radars, and 8,526 antiaircraft guns ultimately dedicated to defend the bridgeheads. Operations over Germany by the bombers and fighters of the Western Allies also disrupted the Luftwaffe effort. P-51s of the US 357th Fighter Group destroyed ten new-production Mistels at Kamenz airfield in March before they could be delivered to KG 200, and a US bomber raid on Parchim airfield on April 7 destroyed four Mistels and 26 other aircraft. Three days later, a B-17 raid on the KG 200 base at Burg, part of a series of attacks on Luftwaffe airfields around Berlin, destroyed five Mistels and damaged hangars, taxiways, and runways. The heavy and unwieldy Mistels were forced to take off while trying to maneuver around craters as they attempted to lift off from damaged runways. Helbig was critical of KG 30, the other unit employing the Mistel, noting they lacked the training KG 200 had undergone in preparation for Operation *Eisenhammer*. KG 30(J)'s maintenance was poor, and several of their Mistels crashed when the tires – which had not rotated as the heavy composite bombers sat idle for months – burst on the runway. The Luftwaffe persisted in the attacks even after the beginning of the Soviet offensive against Berlin, and the last sortie was launched on April 30. The poor reliability and vulnerability of the Mistel and Soviet bridge repair capabilities limited the impact of the Luftwaffe's last major offensive action. Despite the attacks, major damage had only been achieved against the Steinau bridge and, on April 16, the rail bridge at Kustrin.

Konigsberg: the fall of the fortress

Konigsberg had been one of the primary Soviet objectives throughout 1945. After Chernyakovsky's 3rd Belarussian Front broke through German defenses in East Prussia in January, it attacked the city, but German reinforcements allowed the fortress to hold out

German Mistels at an airfield after capture. The Mistel in the foreground does not have the fighter mounted. Craters are visible in the background – German airfields, including those serving as Mistel bases, were heavily attacked by bombers and fighters of the Western Allies in April. (Getty Images)

until April. Chernyakovsky was mortally wounded by German artillery fire on February 18, and three days later Marshal Aleksandr Vasilevsky arrived from his position as Chief of the General Staff to lead the 3rd Belarussian Front's final attacks. The Soviet offensives into East Prussia and Pomerania had pushed back German forces into coastal pockets in Konigsberg, to the north on the Samland Peninsula, and immediately to the south in the Heiligenbeil Cauldron. Luftwaffenkommando Ostpreussen under General Klaus Uebe provided air support to the isolated forces, but his command was reduced to 60 operational aircraft by the beginning of March. Vasilevsky determined to destroy German forces in sequence – first the Cauldron, then Konigsberg, and finally the Samland Peninsula. Soviet forces eliminated the Cauldron's defenders in late March, after which Vasilevsky began to prepare for the attack on Konigsberg.

The Wehrmacht had built four separate lines of fortifications to defend the city, with the 19th-century circle of forts strengthened with newly constructed field fortifications. Vasilevsky massed three armies around for the assault, while two others would pin the German forces on the Samland Peninsula. Aviation support for the attack was unprecedented, including two air armies – the 1st and 3rd – reinforced by bomber corps drawn from the 4th and 15th Air Armies, 500 bombers from the 18th Air Army, and the aircraft of the Baltic Fleet. VVS commander-in-chief Marshal Novikov had arrived with Vasilevsky in late February with a staff operations group drawn from the VVS high command to coordinate the operations of the 2,444 combat aircraft ultimately dedicated to the assault on the city.

Aviation dedicated to the reduction of Konigsberg, April 1945								
Formation	Commander	Light -day bombers	Ground assault	Fighters	Torpedo planes	Heavy bombers	Light -night bombers	Total
1st Air Army	Khryukin	199	319	510			88	1,116
3rd Air Army	Papivin	59	100	240			104	503
18th Air Army	Golovanov	·				500		500
5th Guards Bomber Corps/4th Air Army	Borisenko	72		40				112
5th Guards Bomber Corps/15th Air Army	Ushakov	72						72
Baltic Fleet Aviation	Samokhin	30	60	40	20			150
Total		432	479	830	20	500	192	2,453
Percentages		17.7	19.3	34.1	0.8	20.5	7.6	100

Soviet planners estimated that they outnumbered the small remaining Luftwaffe forces in the area by between 12 and 15 to one, and Vasilevsky planned to rely heavily on his aviation assets to crack the German defenses. Papivin's 3rd Air Army would support the 5th and 39th Armies as they held the German Samland forces in check, in particular suppressing German long-range artillery positions to keep them from interfering with the assault against Konigsberg. Khryukin's 1,116 aircraft would prepare the way with two days of air strikes hitting strongpoints in the main zones of advance, covering the assembly of the attacking armies and suppressing enemy artillery. Given the limited Luftwaffe opposition, many fighters were to be used for ground attack missions, and Colonel F. I. Shinkarenko's 130th Fighter Division was to use its new model Yak-9s with internal bomb bays for the attack. Baltic Fleet aircraft were assigned to interdict any German maritime operations. The Soviets planned to use 5,316 sorties to deliver 2,690 tons of bombs before the attack, and 4,124 sorties on the first day. Operations would then be adjusted as the assault developed.

A VVS regiment prepares for takeoff. By late February, the Soviet situation had improved as better airbases were established, some with concrete runways, and VVS logistics improved. The Luftwaffe efforts to support their forces fighting on the Oder, and strike Soviet-held bridges over the river, would now encounter much heavier Soviet opposition in the air. (Courtesy of the Central Museum of the Armed Forces, Moscow via www.Stavka.photos)

Given the number of aviation formations operating in such a limited area, Novikov's staff arranged precise take-off and landing times and altitudes for ingress and egress, and each air division was assigned its own corridor and specific altitudes. Front-line troops were ordered to mark their forward lines with fires, and intersecting searchlight beams pointed the way at night to the enemy-held center of the city. Aviation staff groups were attached to the command posts of each of the three attacking armies for coordination purposes, and air officers with mobile radio equipment operated with ground force elements to call in air strikes as needed. Novikov established his VVS coordination staff along with the command post of the 43rd Army on the northern attack axis. The post contained bunkers and two observation towers, one of which was used by the advance command element of the 1st Air Army.

Air support was considered essential to the attack, and poor weather on April 1 led Vasilevsky to delay the start of artillery and air preparations. Stalin urged haste due to the upcoming Berlin offensive, and the preliminary bombardment began the next day. At an April 4 conference, weather forecasts led the day of the assault to be postponed from the 5th to the 6th. Despite the meteorologists' predictions, rain and fog persisted and limited the night raids to 766 sorties, mostly by Pe-2 bombers. The assault kicked off on the morning of the 6th, and the Soviets managed to fly 1,052 of the planned 4,000 sorties, most after the weather cleared by midday. The ground forces made good progress, breaking through the outer perimeter defenses. The 11th Guards Army, attacking from the south, secured the railway station and the attack from the north cut off the city from the German forces still holding out on the Samland Peninsula.

April 7 brought improved flying weather, and the VVS was able to at last bring its full power to bear. At 0800hrs, groups of seven to nine aircraft were hitting enemy antiaircraft positions and personnel, while ground attack aircraft struck Luftwaffe airfields. With opposition suppressed, at 1000hrs Novikov ordered 246 Tu-2s of the 334th Bomber Division, escorted by 124 fighters, to launch three waves of strikes aimed at helping the 43rd and 11th Guards Armies break through the particularly strong resistance they faced north of the railroad yards. To the north, 100 bombers dropped 64 tons of ordnance on Pillau, the one remaining port available for the Samland group, followed by two mass strikes by Baltic Fleet aviation delivering another 75 tons of bombs. With German forces still fighting in the city's precincts, the 18th VA was ordered to attack at 1300hrs. Daylight raids by Soviet bomber forces had been virtually unknown since the massive losses suffered in 1941, and Marshal Golovanov, commander of the 18th Air Army, objected to Novikov. The VVS commander-in-chief assured him the bombers would encounter no opposition, as 125 fighters from frontal aviation would fly escort, a further 108 maintained a constant patrol over the city, and 300 Il-2s and Pe-2s would hit German airfields 20 minutes before the attack. The 516 bombers of the 18th Air Army – 330 Il-4s, 58 B-25s, 18 Yer-2s, and 110 Il-2Ms – dropped 3,743 bombs amounting to 550 tons on Konigsberg, without suffering a single loss. Novikov's night bombers followed, beginning at twilight, flying 1,800 sorties delivering another 569 tons of bombs on the battered defenders.

Soviet massed air raid on Konigsberg, 7 April, 1945

On the second day of the Soviet assault on Konigsberg, the weather finally cleared and Air Force commander-in-chief and air coordinator for the operation, Marshal Novikov, ordered a maximum effort against the city. The long-range bombers of the 18th Air Army were typically only used during the hours of night, and for their protection during the daylight raid on April 7, 118 Il-2 Shturmoviks and Pe-2s attacked German airfield and antiaircraft defenses before the raid, with 124 fighters flying escort. Over 500 18th Air Army bombers were able to deliver 550 tons of bombs without loss. The illustration shows two Shtumoviks departing the area after delivering strikes on enemy antiaircraft positions while 18th Air Army DB-3s deliver their bombs on Konigsberg. The 1st, 3rd, and 18th Air Armies and support aircraft of the Baltic Fleet were able to deliver 550 tons of bombs on Konigsberg before its capture on April 10.

Jim Laurier

OPPOSITE THE BERLIN OFFENSIVE, APRIL 1945

April 8 began with more sorties and artillery fire as the attacking Soviet armies committed their second-echelon divisions to keep up the pressure. The Konigsberg port, four forts, and the rail yards were completely secured, and to the west the 5th and 39th Armies drove back the German Samland group by 2km. Soviet aviation flew more than 6,000 sorties, dropping 2,099 tons of bombs on Konigsberg and Pillau. A few scattered Luftwaffe fighters tried to intercept the masses of Soviet aircraft, and Lieutenant Wilhelm Hubner of JG 51, a 62-victory ace, was shot down and killed during the day. On the 9th and 10th, Soviet troops dug out diehard resisters in the ruins of the city and assembled 92,000 prisoners. A final prize, the Kriegsmarine's heavy cruiser *Seydlitz*, slated earlier in the war to be rebuilt as a Kriegsmarine aircraft carrier, was found capsized in Konigsberg's harbor.

The unprecedented massing of aviation resources had made a critical contribution to the Soviet success, helping Vasilevsky take in four days a fortress that had held out for two months. Novikov's pilots had flown 14,090 sorties and dropped 4,440 tons of bombs during the assault, while also neutralizing German forces on the Samland Peninsula and hunting down the few remaining German aircraft in East Prussia. The last German fighter in East Prussia was shot down on April 12, and the 65,000-strong German Samland group totally destroyed on the 21st.

Berlin: The final offensive

Forces and plans

The strategic situation in Europe changed dramatically while Stalin's forces were securing their flanks in Silesia and Pomerania. The Western Allies were across the Rhine by the end of March and encircling the Ruhr. Meanwhile, US forces were advancing rapidly towards

A Soviet photo – probably a composite of one or more separate photos – that reflects the immense concentration of Soviet airpower over Konigsberg. The shot includes Yak-9D fighters passing a lend-lease Boston medium bomber. The attack on Konigsberg integrated aircraft from two frontal air armies and the Baltic Fleet, and on April 7 included a rare daytime raid on the long-range bombers of the 18th Air Army. (Courtesy of the Central Museum of the Armed Forces, Moscow via www.Stavka.photos)

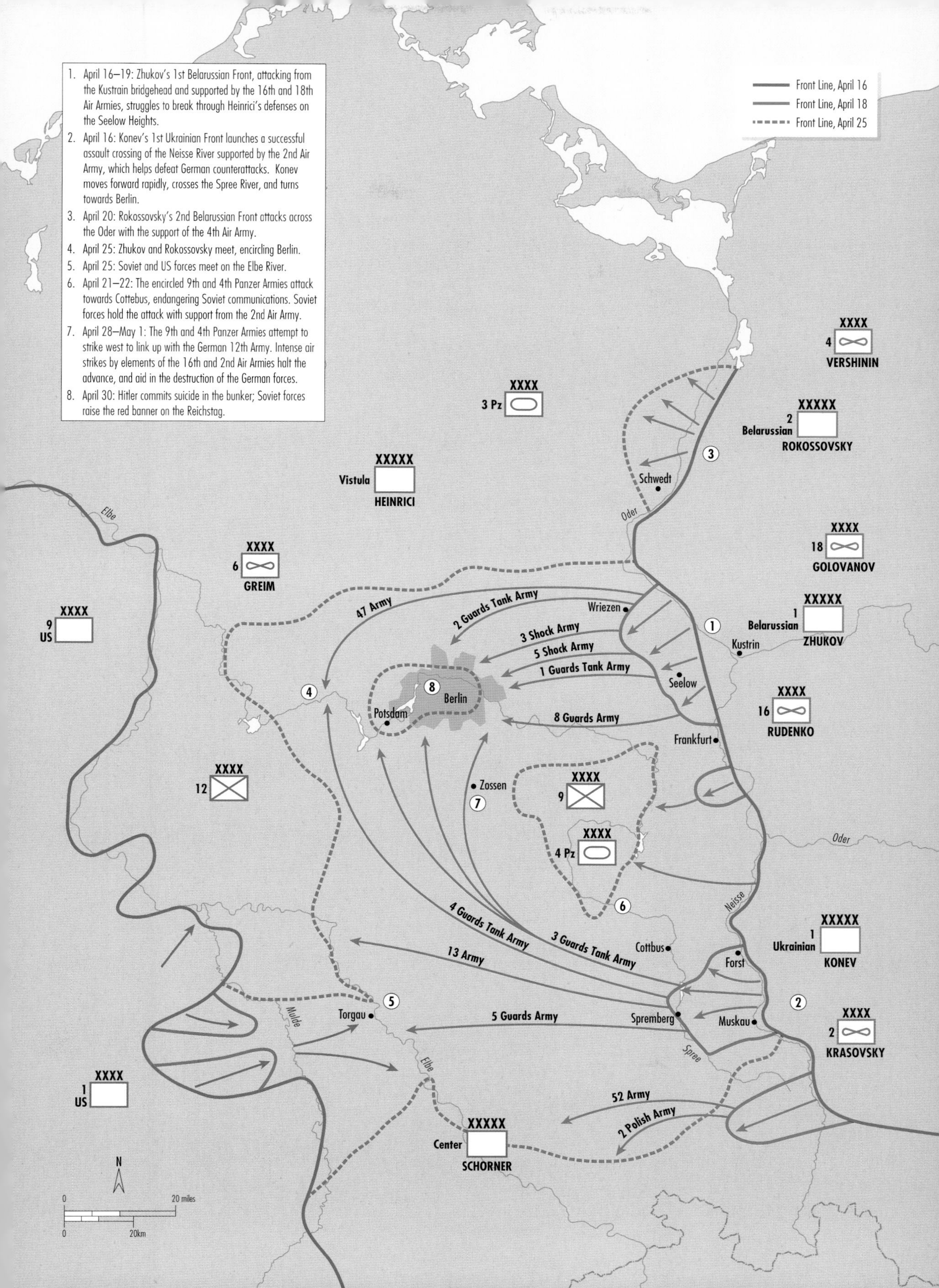
1. April 16–19: Zhukov's 1st Belarussian Front, attacking from the Kustrain bridgehead and supported by the 16th and 18th Air Armies, struggles to break through Heinrici's defenses on the Seelow Heights.
2. April 16: Konev's 1st Ukrainian Front launches a successful assault crossing of the Neisse River supported by the 2nd Air Army, which helps defeat German counterattacks. Konev moves forward rapidly, crosses the Spree River, and turns towards Berlin.
3. April 20: Rokossovsky's 2nd Belarussian Front attacks across the Oder with the support of the 4th Air Army.
4. April 25: Zhukov and Rokossovsky meet, encircling Berlin.
5. April 25: Soviet and US forces meet on the Elbe River.
6. April 21–22: The encircled 9th and 4th Panzer Armies attack towards Cottebus, endangering Soviet communications. Soviet forces hold the attack with support from the 2nd Air Army.
7. April 28–May 1: The 9th and 4th Panzer Armies attempt to strike west to link up with the German 12th Army. Intense air strikes by elements of the 16th and 2nd Air Armies halt the advance, and aid in the destruction of the German forces.
8. April 30: Hitler commits suicide in the bunker; Soviet forces raise the red banner on the Reichstag.
Front Line, April 16
Front Line, April 18
Front Line, April 25
XXXX 4 VERSHININ
XXXX 3 Pz
XXXXX 2 Belarussian ROKOSSOVSKY
XXXXX Vistula HEINRICI
Schwedt
Oder
Elbe
XXXX 18 GOLOVANOV
XXXX 6 GREIM
XXXXX 1 Belarussian ZHUKOV
XXXX 9 US
47 Army
2 Guards Tank Army
Wriezen
3 Shock Army
5 Shock Army
1 Guards Tank Army
Kustrin
Seelow
Berlin
Potsdam
8 Guards Army
XXXX 16 RUDENKO
Frankfurt
XXXX 12
Zossen
XXXX 9
XXXX 4 Pz
Oder
Neisse
4 Guards Tank Army
3 Guards Tank Army
13 Army
Cottbus
XXXXX 1 Ukrainian KONEV
Forst
Mulde
Torgau
5 Guards Army
Spremberg
Muskau
XXXX 2 KRASOVSKY
Spree
Elbe
XXXX 1 US
52 Army
2 Polish Army
XXXXX Center SCHORNER
N
0
20 miles
0
20km

the Elbe, the agreed delineation line for the meeting of Soviet and Western Allied forces, heightening Stalin's fears that his allies would make a dash to seize Berlin. On April 1, Stalin informed Eisenhower that Hitler's capital was now of secondary significance, and the Red Army would attack only in May and to the south of the city. In reality, the Stavka began intense planning the same day for an immediate offensive to seize Berlin. Soviet planners estimated that it would take 12–15 days to encircle and capture the capital. To spur on his marshals in the attack, Stalin left open the question of who would take Berlin, giving Konev hopes of beating Zhukov to the Reichstag even though his start-lines on the Neisse were far to the south. It took two weeks to redeploy the 1st and 2nd Belarussian Fronts and 1st Ukrainian Front to their assault positions. Konev shifted the main weight of his force from Silesia to the Neisse River line, and Rokossovsky, still completing operations around Danzig, began a rapid deployment west to take over the northern Oder River line front from Zhukov. Konev and Zhukov were ready to launch the offensive on April 16; Rokossovsky would attack four days later.

Three fronts supported by four air armies with 7,200 combat aircraft would make the assault. The ground forces totaled 2.5 million men, 6,250 tanks and self-propelled guns, and over 40,000 artillery pieces. Zhukov had the advantage of his now-consolidated Kustrin bridgehead over the Oder, while Konev and Rokossovsky would have to launch assault crossings over the Neisse and northern Oder Rivers. Rudenko's 16th Air Army was attached to Zhukov, Krasovsky's 2nd Air Army to Konev, and Vershinin's 4th Air Army to Rokossovsky. Preparations were extensive, with 290 airfields constructed or renovated in the rear areas and stocked with fuel and ammunition. Airfields could be positioned close to the front line due to Soviet air dominance, allowing for rapid turn-around and increased sortie rates. Rudenko was augmented by an aviation corps from the Stavka reserve and fielded 3,188 combat aircraft, while Krasovsky's had 2,148 combat aircraft and Vershinin 1,360. The long-range

Bombs ready for loading at a Pe-2 base. Despite some Tu-2s entering the operational force in 1945, the majority of frontal air army light bomber divisions still flew the Pe-2s when Berlin fell.

bombers of Golovanov's 18th Air Army shifted from the Konigsberg area to support the 1st Belarussian Front's attack. About 30 aircraft were available for each kilometer of front, with 100 per kilometer in major attack sectors. In the 5th Shock Army and 8th Guards Army sectors of Zhukov's front, selected as the primary breakthrough zone, the ratio approached 170–200 aircraft per kilometer. Rokossovsky was particularly dependent on air support as much of his artillery would still be in transit during the first days of his attack.

The number of aircraft and aviation units exceeded even those in the Konigsberg operation, and Novikov established his headquarters with the 16th Air Army command post to coordinate the four air armies involved. VVS planning for the air offensive was once again rigorously focused on tactical support to the attacking fronts. Shturmovik and army units were paired before the offensive, allowing air and ground officers to establish personal contact and coordinate plans. Aviation liaison elements assigned to operate with the ground forces were well equipped with short-wave radios to ensure close air–ground cooperation. The joint planning with ground staffs included the seizure of German airfields by the exploiting tank armies, and airbase engineering and service battalions were to follow close behind their advanced guards. Rudenko's 16th Air Army alone had 16,600 tons of ammunition and 15,300 tons of fuel at its bases to support the offensive. A fleet of 420 petrol bowsers divided into convoys of 15–20 vehicles was ready to transport 920 tons of fuel to captured airfields. The 16th Air Army flew 2,600 recon sorties and mapped German defenses to a depth of 60km. The entire area was photographed twice, and key attack axes eight times. Novikov and his air army commanders would use the sophisticated radar network established along the front – for the first time operating in a fully integrated fashion – to assist in controlling VVS operations.

The VVS Berlin Offensive operation							
Air armies	Total aircraft	Front supported	Fighters	Assault	Day bombers	Night bombers	Recon/ Spotters
4th VA	1,360	2nd Belarussian	602	449	146	137	26
16th VA	3,188	1st Belarussian	1,567	731	762		128
2nd VA	2,148	1st Ukrainian	1,106	529	422		91
Totals	6,696		3,275	1,709	1,330	137	245

Each of the air army plans was tailored to the requirements of their specific fronts. Zhukov's 1st Belarussian Front massed his main attack force in the Kustrin bridgehead, and 2,453 of Rudenko's aircraft were to support the primary assault against German forces blocking the road to Berlin. The majority of the 16th Air Army's units, including eight air corps and seven independent air divisions, supported the zone of attack of the 5th Shock Army, 8th Guards Army and two tank armies. Bombers of the 18th Air Army were to launch massed night bomber attacks against the German defenses on the Seelow Heights. Rudenko allocated just a single air division each to support Zhukov's secondary attacks to the north and south. The 2nd Air Army only moved its aircraft to its forward bases two days before the offensive to conceal Konev's main axes of attack. Konev's river crossing would be supported by four attack waves of 800, 570, 430, and 370 planes, with smaller groupings of mixed plane types keeping up the pressure between the massed strikes. Vershinin planned 4,000 sorties for the first day of Rokossovsky's offensive to compensate for the 2nd Belarussian Front's lack of artillery. Due to its small bomber force, the 4th Air Army would make more extensive use of its Shturmoviks in deep raids to suppress enemy artillery during the front's river crossing.

Despite the Soviet presence on the Oder since February, Hitler had been slow to strengthen the front or order Berlin prepared for defense, and dispatched his last strategic reserve, the

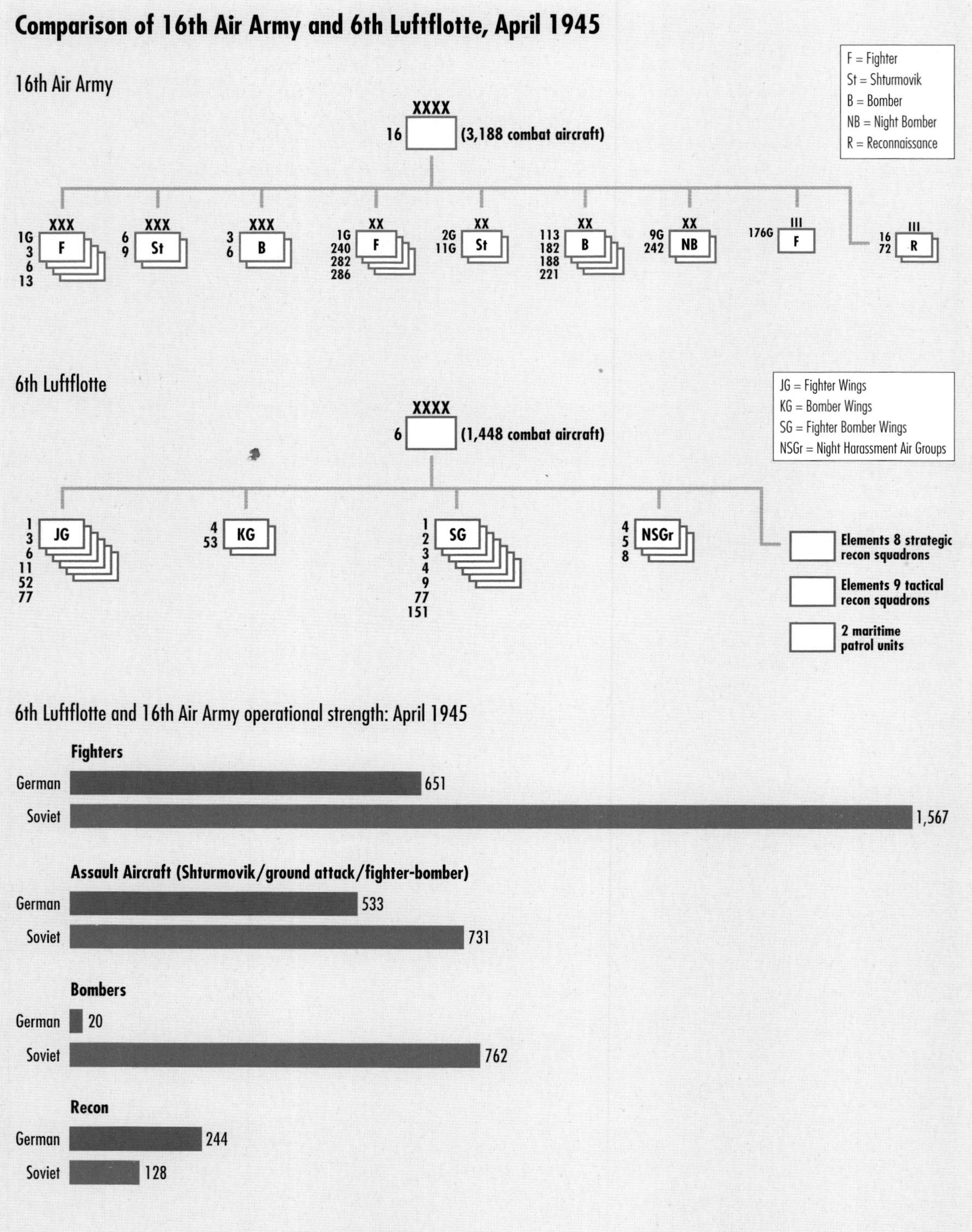

Comparison of 16th Air Army and 6th Luftflotte, April 1945
16th Air Army
F = Fighter
St = Shturmovik
B = Bomber
NB = Night Bomber
R = Reconnaissance
XXXX
16
(3,188 combat aircraft)
XXX
1G 3 6 13
F
XXX
6 9
St
XXX
3 6
B
XX
1G 240 282 286
F
XX
2G 11G
St
XX
113 182 188 221
B
XX
9G 242
NB
III
176G
F
III
16 72
R
6th Luftflotte
JG = Fighter Wings
KG = Bomber Wings
SG = Fighter Bomber Wings
NSGr = Night Harassment Air Groups
XXXX
6
(1,448 combat aircraft)
1 3 6 11 52 77
JG
4 53
KG
1 2 3 4 9 77 151
SG
4 5 8
NSGr
Elements 8 strategic recon squadrons
Elements 9 tactical recon squadrons
2 maritime patrol units
6th Luftflotte and 16th Air Army operational strength: April 1945
Fighters
German 651
Soviet 1,567
Assault Aircraft (Shturmovik/ground attack/fighter-bomber)
German 533
Soviet 731
Bombers
German 20
Soviet 762
Recon
German 244
Soviet 128

OPPOSITE COMPARISON OF 16TH AIR ARMY AND LUFTFLOTTE 6, APRIL 1945

This graphic compares the organization and strength of the VVS 16th Air Army and Luftwaffe Luftflotte 6 before the Berlin offensive in April 1945. Rudenko's air army heavily outnumbered Greim's Luftflotte 6, and in addition Greim had to face the bombers of the 18th Air Army and 4th Air Army to the north and 2nd Air Army to the south. Fuel shortages further reduced the number of aircraft the Luftwaffe could sortie each day. The 16th Air Army particularly outnumbered the German fighter force in the East, and the Luftwaffe had largely disbanded its bombers with the exception of KG 200's small force of Mistel composite bombers.

Soviet air units were concentrated in corps and divisions and attached to specific ground armies to allow for effective direct support. Luftwaffe *Geschwaders* (air wings) were more flexibly organized, and could be rapidly shifted to serve under a variety of *Fliegerkorps* (air corps), *Fliegerdivisions* (air divisions), or *Luftwaffenkommands* (air force commands) to respond to the developing situation.

6th SS Panzer Army, to launch an offensive towards Budapest. By the middle of March, the Fuhrer finally began to consider measures to protect the capital and ordered the preparation of a series of defensive lines around the city. Almost 3,000 Luftwaffe aircraft were available on the Eastern Front in early April, but the intense air operations in February and March had severely reduced fuel reserves. Luftwaffe leaders estimated there was only enough fuel to keep a tenth of that number flying, and Luftflotte 6 disbanded six fighter groups in March. Luftflotte 6 thus faced the four attacking VVS air armies in early April with 1,524 operational combat aircraft. On April 12, Luftwaffenkommando Nordost under General Martin Fiebig was established to command German air assets supporting Army Group Vistula. Fiebig was reinforced with Sondergruppe A, a suicide unit with 100 aircraft, and Fighter Division 1, with 300 fighters including some Me 262 jets. The Luftwaffe had another 306 fighters, 339 fighter bombers, 35 bombers, and 111 reconnaissance aircraft to oppose Konev's attack over the Neisse. Almost all available fuel reserves went to Greim for the final defense of the city. Two hundred Flak batteries had been moved to the front line to face Zhukov's and Konev's troops, while 600 Flak guns were still defending Berlin itself and would be used against attacking Soviet armor. Berlin was garrisoned by the LVI Panzer Corps with six divisions and 50 Volkssturm battalions.

Luftflotte 6 serviceable aircraft totals, January–April 1945		
	Luftflotte 6, January	Luftflotte 6, April
Fighters	153	641
Night fighters	76	
Bombers	10	20
Ground attack	278	533
Night ground attack	47	86
Strategic recon	88	59
Tactical recon	143	185
Transports	27	
Totals	822	1,524
KG 200 (Special Operations)	206	70

The breakthrough – April 16–19

Zhukov massed 10,000 guns to bombard German lines in the early morning of the 16th and positioned 143 searchlights from the Moscow air defense system to blind the enemy as his infantry attacked. The 1st Belarussian Front alone included 768,000 troops, 3,000 tanks, and 14,000 guns, heavily outnumbering the opposing German 9th Army's 220,000 troops and 512 tanks. At 0430hrs, 109 of Rudenko's night bombers attacked identified German headquarters and line of communication targets 10–12km behind the front line. Half an hour later, green flares signaled the beginning of Zhukov's artillery barrage. The 18th Air Army simultaneously struck a series of key defensive positions and line of communication targets with 743 bombers, dropping 924 tons of ordnance in 42 minutes. The artillery barrage was massive but largely wasted, as Heinrici had pulled back all but light screening forces from his forward line of defense. Furthermore, the searchlights were reflected by the clouds of smoke and hindered the attacking troops more than the enemy, and German troops on the Seelow Heights rained down fire on the Soviet first-echelon divisions struggling through the marshy terrain below. Rudenko had planned a mass raid of 730 ground attack aircraft and 455 bombers for the early hours of the attack, but morning fog and fires and smoke from the barrage limited the ability of Soviet aircraft to identify targets. For some hours, VVS air support was confined to small groups of between six and nine Shturmoviks prowling over the front to hit any German positions that became visible. Rudenko gave orders that Il-2Ms returning from strikes that found their home bases fogged in were to land on any clear airfield to be refueled and rearmed. By 0800hrs, conditions began to clear and Pe-2 dive-bombers were able to join in the attack. Infuriated by the slow progress, Zhukov committed his 1st and 2nd Guards Tank Armies before the first-echelon armies had secured a breakthrough. Some 1,300 tanks and self-propelled guns, along with thousands of trucks and support vehicles, poured into the crowded bridgehead between the Oder and the Seelow Heights, creating a tremendous traffic jam and offering even more targets for the heavy German fire.

Air activity intensified as Luftwaffe aircraft arrived over the battle zone. Rudenko's aircraft were ordered to drop their bomb loads on any likely German positions if unable to identify their pre-planned targets. By 1500hrs, the weather had cleared and 647 of Rudenko's aircraft were in the air, on call to support ground units. The 5th Shock Army's 80th Rifle Corps called on the 198th Guards Ground Attack Division to suppress German artillery halting its advance, and the Shturmoviks formed a battle circle above the enemy guns. The Il-2Ms dove from the circle in sequence, kept the artillerymen in their shelters, and hit targets less

A confident VVS fighter pilot on the wing of his Lavochkin fighter. After the disappointing LaGG-3 and initial La-5 fighers, the Lavochkin Design Bureau produced the La-5FN and La-7 fighters, with powerful radial engines. The La series were the Soviet answer to the Fw 190, and the La-7 was in particular superior to all but the very latest version of the German fighter. (Courtesy of the Central Museum of the Armed Forces, Moscow via www.Stavka.photos)

A formation of Soviet Pe-2 light bombers on a mission. Pe-2 were particularly effective in suppressing German artillery during Konev's and Rokossovsky's river crossing operations on the 16th and 20th of April. (Courtesy of the Central Museum of the Armed Forces, Moscow via www.Stavka.photos)

than 300 meters from the lead troops. Fighters on both sides scored kills. JG 11 Fw 190s caught a formation of A-20s returning from a strike and shot down four, with Feldwebel Paul Berndt – who had shot down a Pe-2 earlier in the day – claiming three of the A-20s. Captain Sergey Morgunov of the 15th Fighter Regiment in turn downed three Fw 190s in his Yak-3, bringing his total score to 36. The high-scoring La-7s of the 176th Guards Fighter Regiment reported shooting down 16 Fw 190s in ten air engagements without suffering any losses. The 16th and 18th Air Armies had flown a combined total of 6,110 sorties on the first day of the offensive despite the difficult weather, delivering 1,514 tons of bombs, but Zhukov's forces were still stalled in front of the Seelow Heights as night fell. When evening aerial reconnaissance identified German troops moving from Berlin to the battle area, 255 of the 18th Air Army's Il-4s hit four road intersections to disorganize their approach, while another 320 of Golovanov's bombers and 138 of Rudenko's night bombers struck enemy headquarters and airfields.

Konev's barrage began at 0615hrs. Krasovsky dedicated 668 sorties to the initial attack, with 208 Pe-2s dive-bombing German front-line defenses at Forst and Muskau, while three groups of nine elite Pe-2 groups each dive-bombed enemy headquarters identified by aerial reconnaissance. Konev's artillery, along with 2nd Air Army Il-2Ms, laid a smoke screen along 420km of the river front to cover the first waves of assault boats. The 1st Ukrainian Front troops launched 160 attacks across the river, but although 133 were successful the crossings faced rapid counterattacks and had to call in air support. Near Forst, 85 Il-2s from the 2nd Guards Ground Attack Regiment and 25 Il-10s of the 108th Guards Ground Attack Regiment, escorted by 50 fighters, hit a counterattacking German force, while the 1st Guards Ground Attack Corps sent 100 Il-2s, escorted by 65 fighters, to suppress enemy artillery positions around Muskau. The Luftwaffe flew 453 sorties against Konev, 220 by fighter bombers that delivered 74 tons of bombs and 408 Panzerblitz rockets against the bridgeheads, but at the end of the day the 1st Ukrainian Front had 22 bridges, ten ferries, and 28 smaller storming bridges in operation. The 60-ton bridges allowed tanks to cross and

2nd Air Army support to 1st Ukrainian Front assault across the Neisse River

Spree River

10

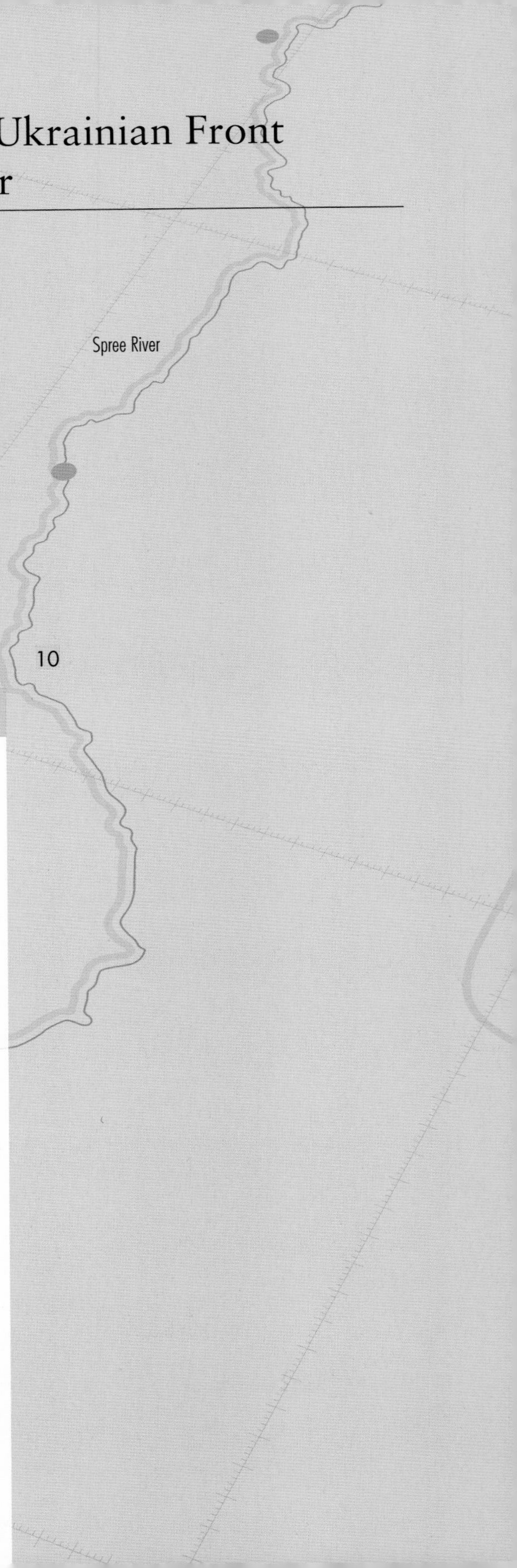

EVENTS

1. 208 Pe-2 light bombers from the 6th Guards and 4th Bomber Corps strike Forst and Muskau immediately before the assault.

2. Il-2s aid the artillery in laying a 420km smokescreen covering the infantry assault across the Neisse River.

3. As the bombardment ends, the 2nd Guards Air Assault Corps (170 Il-2), 2nd Fighter Corps (160 fighters), 6th Guards Bomber Corps fly to strike enemy defenses in support of the 3rd Shock Army.

4. Simultaneously, the 1st Guards Air Assault Corps (160 Il-2), 6th Guards Fighter (260 fighters), 4th Bomber Corps (120 Pe-2) strikes enemy defenses in support of the 13th and 5th Guards.

5. German forces counterattack, near Forst, 85 Il-2s from the 2nd Guards Air Assault Corps and 25 Il-10s from the 108th Guards Air Assault Regiment escorted by 50 fighters strike counterattacking units and their supporting artillery.

6. To the south, German artillery positions supporting counterattacks are struck by 100 Il-2s of the 1st Guards Air Assault Corps escorted by 65 fighters.

7. On the secondary axis to the south, the 3rd Air Assault Corps (90 Il-2) and 5th Fighter Corps (90 fighters) support the 52nd and 2nd Polish Armies with 306 sorties.

8. The lead elements of the 3rd and 4th Guards Tank Armies begin to cross the heavy pontoon bridges over the Neisse.

9. By evening, Konev's 1st Ukrainian Front has established its bridgehead and penetrated the second "Matilda" line of defense.

10. By April 18th, the 1st Ukrainian Front will be across the Spree River and ready to turn north to attack Berlin from the south.

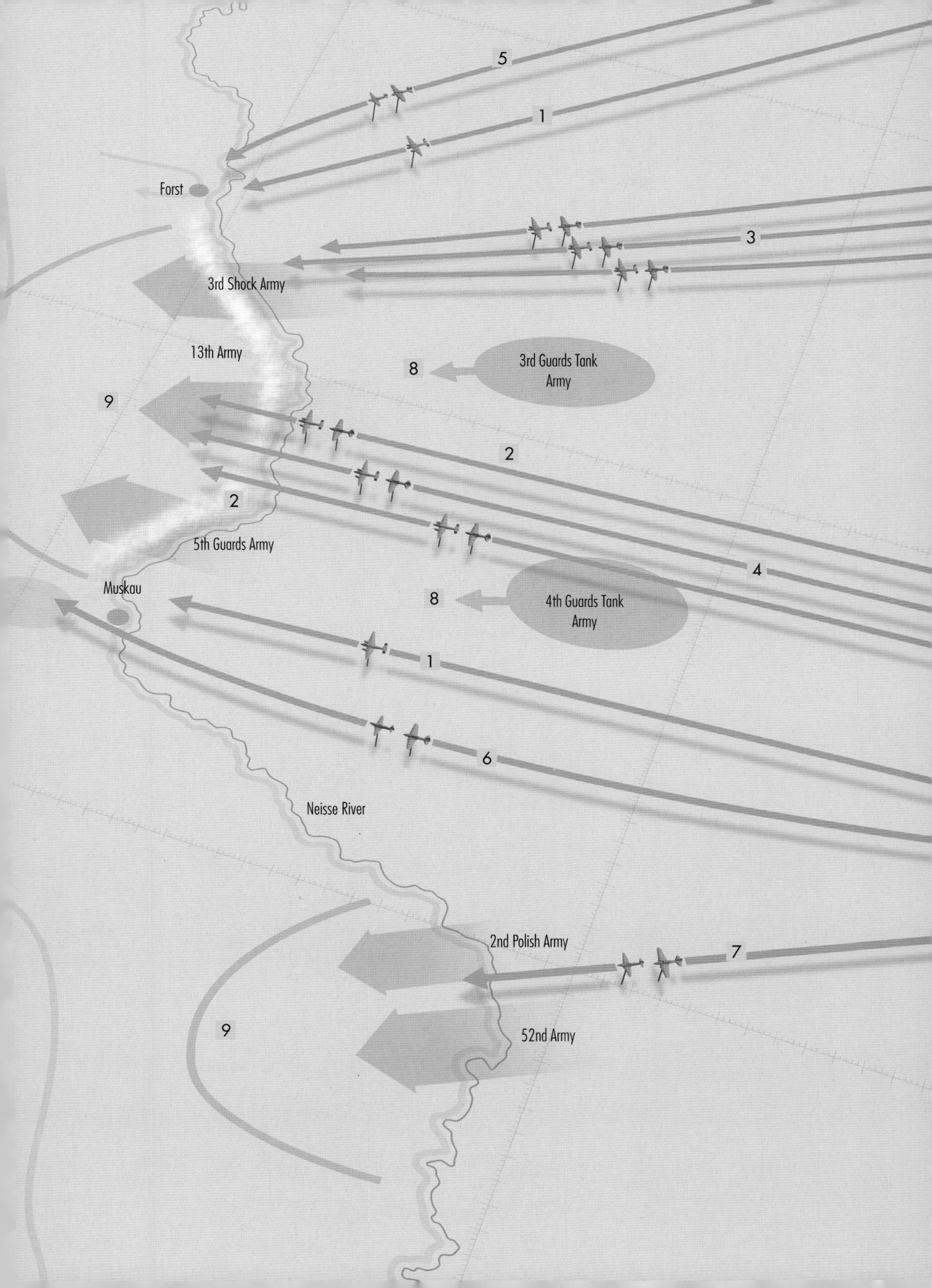

5
1
Forst
3
3rd Shock Army
13th Army
8
3rd Guards Tank Army
9
2
2
5th Guards Army
4
Muskau
8
4th Guards Tank Army
1
6
Neisse River
2nd Polish Army
7
9
52nd Army

A Luftwaffe Fw 190 in flight. German airmen contested the Soviet advance on Berlin, even managing some sorties as the city center was being assaulted, until their airbases were overrun by ground forces. (Nik Cornish at www.Stavka.photos)

advance as deep as 10km into German defenses. Krasovsky's 2nd Air Army had flown a total of 3,546 sorties and claimed 40 German planes shot down in 33 air engagements. Konev's 3rd and 4th Guards Tank Armies were able to enter the battle on the afternoon of April 17.

The Luftwaffe flew a total of 891 sorties over both the Oder and Neisse battle zones on the first day of the Soviet offensive, claiming 125 aerial victories, and KG 200 launched another Mistel attack against the railroad bridge at Kustrin. Novikov used his radar network to intercept the 20–40-strong Luftwaffe fighter bomber formations as they approached the edge of the battle area. Rudenko's 3rd Fighter Corps alone claimed 50 Luftwaffe aircraft downed while covering the 5th Shock Army, and the 16th Air Army reported downing a total of 165, at a cost of 87 aircraft lost. Krasovsky's airmen claimed an additional 40 victories over the Neisse River battlefield.

In the early morning of April 17, 766 18th Air Army bombers returned to drop 931 tons of bombs on the German defenses around Seelow. The flying weather was poor this day, particularly in the 1st Belarussian Front's zone, but Rudenko's airmen were still able to claim 46 kills. Ivan Kozhedub and his wingman from the La-7-equipped 176th Guards Fighter Regiment intercepted a formation of 40 Fw 190 fighter bombers and Kozhedub shot down two, bringing his final wartime tally to 62. To the south, the Luftwaffe's efforts to hit Konev's tanks as they crossed the river were intercepted by 2nd Air Army fighter cover, the 6th Guards Fighter Corps claiming 48 kills.

Zhukov's forces fought their way atop the Seelow Heights on April 18 – at last taking their first day objectives – but the 1st Belarussian Front had still not achieved a clean breakthrough. A massive dogfight developed over Zhukov's battle lines as the Luftwaffe again flew a maximum effort, claiming to shoot down 169 VVS aircraft. JG 6 flew 64 sorties and claimed 23 kills for the loss of ten Fw 190s, while JG 11 reported 40 victories. Two VVS aces – Captain Ivan Landik of the La-7-equipped 482nd Fighter Regiment, with 18 victories, and Senior Lieutenant Petr Guchyok of the Aircobra-equipped 100th Guards Fighter Regiment, with 16 kills – were shot down and killed during the air battle. Rudenko's airmen also scored successes, claiming 151 of the 218 Luftwaffe aircraft reported shot down that day. Vectored in by radar guidance and the command post of the 3rd Fighter Corps, eight Yak-9s of the 43rd Fighter Regiment led by Senior Lieutenant Ivan Kuznetsov bounced a formation of Fw 190 fighter bombers during the day, shooting down four and forcing the rest to jettison their bombs. Kuznetsov was responsible for two of the kills and became one of the most successful VVS fighter pilots in the last weeks of the war, downing a total of ten enemy aircraft from April 16–23 to end the war with 26 victories. The Yak-3s of the 233rd Fighter Regiment claimed another ten victories, five by Lietuenant Aleksandr Yersho. A number of other Soviet aces increased their scores on the 18th. Captain Sergey Morgunov claimed four

Fw 190s in his 15th Fighter Regiment Yak-3, raising his total to 40; Captain Vitaliy Popkov of the 5th Guards Fighter Regiment also advanced his score to 40 by shooting down two Fw 190s in his La-7; and Lieutenant Colonel Dmitriy Glinka of the 100th Guards Fighter Regiment increased his score to 49 by destroying two Fw 190s and a Bf 109 in his Aircobra.

The 16th Air Army also flew a large number of ground support sorties on the 18th, and the 108th Guards Attack Regiment – flying new Il-10s – claimed 14 enemy motor vehicles and one tank destroyed in a single mission. The Aircobra-equipped fighters of the 104th Guards Fighter Regiment launched strafing raids on German airfields that destroyed two Me 262 jet fighters of JG-7 on the ground. To the south, the 2nd Air Army supported Konev's tank armies as they crossed the Spree River and began to swing north. The Luftwaffe tried to strike Konev's tank columns with attacks by groups of 24 fighter bombers, but Soviet fighters covered the advance and reported shooting down 67 enemy aircraft. With Konev's strong progress across the Neisse, Stalin authorized him to direct his two tank armies towards Berlin, infuriating Zhukov, whose 1st Belarussian Front was still bogged down on the Seelow Heights. Rudenko and Krasovsky had flown a total of 6,434 sorties on the 18th and claimed 218 enemy aircraft destroyed.

The next day, Zhukov's forces – at a cost of a quarter of his armor and 33,000 killed – at last broke through the German Seelow fortified zone. The 16th and 18th Air Armies had flown 16,442 combat sorties over four days to help break through Heinrici's defenses. Coordination between the tank armies, now able to advance at speed, and the VVS fighters and Shturmoviks overhead was excellent and aviation liaison groups rapidly called in air strikes when the lead tanks met any resistance. VVS fighter regiments covered the advance, and the 16th Air Army claimed 112 German aircraft shot down during April 19, 68 by the Yak-3s and Yak-9s of the 3rd Fighter Corps. The 3rd Fighter Corps' 15th Fighter Regiment had the most success in these engagements, with three of its pilots claiming three victories apiece, and the regiment reporting a total of 19 kills. Six of the 176th Fighter Regiment's La-7s engaged 30 enemy aircraft and claimed to shoot down six Fw 190s without loss the same day.

Encircling the capital, April 20–25

The 2nd Belarussian Front began its attack on April 20. North of Berlin, the Oder was a difficult obstacle, with two branches separated by sandbars and marshy terrain. Vershinin's pilots flew 1,085 sorties to hit German defenses the night before the assault, with the 5th Guards Night Bomber Regiment – a unit manned by female pilots – particularly distinguishing itself. The 4th Air Army had planned on 4,071 sorties for April 20, but the morning dawned with poor weather and Vershinin resorted to flying pairs of Shturmoviks and Pe-2s over the front to search out and strike targets when spotted through the thick mist. Troops that were able to cross the Oder were rapidly threatened by counterattacks supported by heavy German artillery fire from long-range guns at Stettin. As the weather began to clear

Soviet ace Captain I. N. Kozhedub shoots down an Me 262, February 19, 1945

The Luftwaffe retained most of its small number of operational Me 262 jets to oppose US and British strategic bomber attacks, and few were engaged by Soviet pilots. The top Allied ace of the war, however, Captain I. N. Kozhedub, added a Me 262 jet to his total kills on February 19, 1945. Flying with his wingman on a free hunt operation in their La-7 fighters, Kozhedub noticed an aircraft flying back towards German lines near the Oder River. Kozhedub's wingman, Dmitry Titorenko, fired a burst that caused the Me 262 to pull to his left into Kozhedub's line of fire. The Soviet ace noted afterwards that if the German pilot had chosen to fly straight away at maximum speed, the jet would have outrun his La-7. The Me 262 exploded, bringing Kozhedub's score to 55; he would down several more enemy aircraft in the next weeks, with two Fw 190s shot down on April 17 bringing his wartime total to 62. This illustration shows the Me 262 exploding in the sky and being followed by the two La-7 Soviet fighters.

27
Jim Laurier

Soviet fighters taking antiaircraft fire. When Luftwaffe opposition was less in evidence, the VVS would use its fighters for ground attack purposes. (Courtesy of the Central Museum of the Armed Forces, Moscow via www.Stavka.photos)

around 0900hrs, 4th Air Army aircraft swept in to suppress the artillery fire and support the shallow bridgeheads. The 65th Army commander reported that his forces would not have been able to repel the counterattacks without the Shturmoviks. Covered by air, light temporary bridges were thrown across the river in the 65th Army's sector, followed over the next several days by heavier bridges able to support tanks and other heavy equipment.

At the same time, Zhukov's and Konev's lead units were in a race to Berlin. The VVS kept air cover over the advancing tank armies with constant fighter patrols, and radar-vectored interceptors against Luftwaffe attacks. Reconnaissance aircraft scouted ahead of the columns and Il-2s cleared the way for the advance. As Luftwaffe opposition ebbed, the VVS increasingly employed its fighters to strafe enemy positions and columns with machine-gun and cannon fire, rockets, and bombs. The 1st Ukrainian Front struck north from the Spree River, with the 6th Guards Fighter Corps covering the 4th Guards Tank Army and claiming 56 enemy aircraft downed in 50 separate aerial engagements during the exploitation phase. Konev's 3rd Guards Tank Army advanced 60km on April 20, while Zhukov's artillery was finally able to open fire on Berlin's eastern suburbs at around 1100hrs.

The Luftwaffe continued to generate as many sorties as possible, clashing with the VVS fighter cover. JG 6 flew 64 Fw 190 sorties on the 20th, claiming to shoot down two VVS aircraft for the loss of two of its own. The 16th Air Army flew 4,054 combat sorties the same day and claimed to down 90 German aircraft. In one action, 15 Il-2s were attacked by a reported 90 Fw 190s to the northeast of Berlin, but the escorting 14 Aircobras of the 20th Guards Fighter Regiment fended them off, claiming five victories but losing Captain Aleksandr Filatov, a 21-victory ace. One entire four-aircraft *schwarm* from JG 3 led by Feldwebel Willi Maximowitz, a 27-victory ace, was intercepted over Konev's front and shot down by 2nd Air Army fighters.

As the lead elements of the 1st Ukrainian and 1st Belarussian Fronts drove into the city's outskirts, the VVS launched a series of large-scale bomber attacks to pave the way for the assault into the city. During the night of April 20–21, the German defensive positions on the eastern and southeastern edges of Berlin were subjected to a raid by 548 of Golovanov's 18th Air Army bombers and 184 of Rudenko's 16th Air Army Pe-2s. In the early hours of April 25, the 18th Air Army returned with a 111-strong bomber raid aimed at potential strongpoints in Berlin, and the 16th Air Army followed up during the daylight hours with two air strikes totaling 1,368 aircraft. The 18th Air Army completed the sequence with 563 aircraft in a raid on the city during the early morning of April 26. Delayed-action bombs were used to increase the defenders' difficulties.

Flying weather was poor on April 21 and the Soviets claimed only 39 victories in 41 air engagements. Attrition, fuel shortages, and the loss of its bases crippled the Luftwaffe's ability to get aircraft into the air over Berlin. On the 22nd, the 5th Mechanized Corps overran the Juterbog airfield complex, capturing 144 derelict aircraft and an ammunition depot with 3,000 bombs. The 9th Guards Air Regiment deployed forward to operate from the captured base. On April 23, the Luftwaffe mounted sorties to try to protect the remaining open routes into the city to the west, resulting in several air clashes, and the 16th Air Army claimed 25 German aircraft downed. Konev's 3rd Guards Tank Army assaulted the ring road south of the city, led by a 1,420-gun barrage, covered by the 2nd Fighter Corps and supported by strikes by 205 Pe-2s of the 6th Guards Bomber Corps. The Luftwaffe tried to meet the attack, using aircraft from outside Berlin and the detachment of fighters still operating from Templehof, directed by the Luftwaffe detachment operating from the Fuhrerbunker, but the German airmen reported they could not get through the "impenetrable air umbrella" of VVS fighters over the city. In one action, four Yak-3s of the 1st Guards Fighter Regiment were vectored towards eight Fw 190 fighter bombers flying to hit Soviet forces crossing the Teltow Canal. Flying down from 1,300 meters, the Yaks rapidly shot down three of the Fws, forcing the rest to jettison their bombs and flee. During the day, the VVS claimed a total of 75 kills for the loss of just three aircraft. As Konev and Zhukov tightened their grip on the suburbs on the 25th, their spearheads met near Potsdam, encircling the city. The 16th Air Army claimed 20 German aircraft for the loss of 14 the same day. German veteran pilots could still draw blood, and Lieutenant Gunther Josten, recently appointed to command a Gruppe of JG 51, claimed seven victories on April 25 to bring his tally to 178. To the west of the embattled city, elements of the US 1st Army and Konev's 5th Guards Army met at Torgau on the Elbe River the same day.

Pe-2s in formation. Pe-2 dive bombers hit and destroyed a critical bridge west of Warsaw during the Vistula–Oder offensive, stranding a German column of 5,000 vehicles on the road, resulting in repeated attacks by additional VVS strike aircraft. Despite the arrival of the improved Tu-2 later in the war, Soviet light bomber regiments were still predominantly equipped with Pe-2s. (Courtesy of the Central Museum of the Armed Forces, Moscow via www.Stavka.photos)

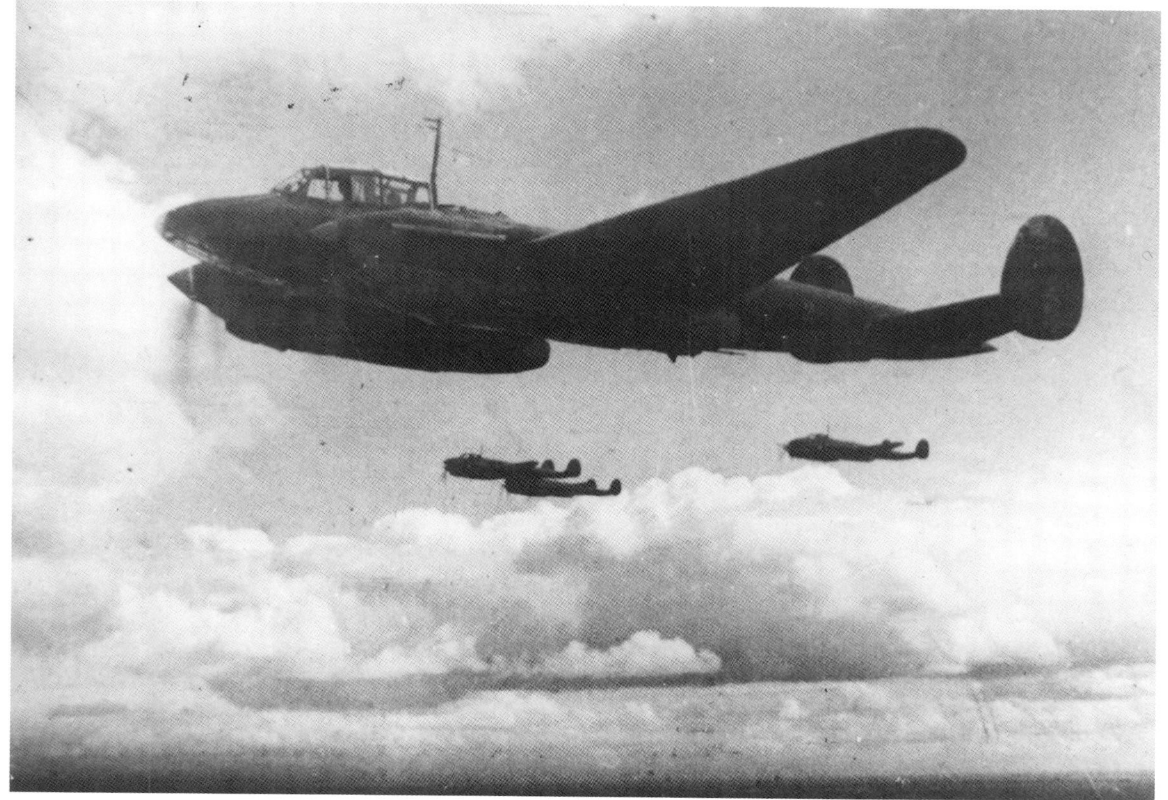

The battle for the Reichstag

Multiple Soviet armies were now attacking towards the center of Berlin, Konev's from the south and Zhukov's from north and east. Due to fires, smoke, and the close-quarters fighting, the VVS operated strike aircraft in small, tightly controlled groups during the battle for the heart of the city. Fighter units patrolled above to intercept any Luftwaffe attempts at resupply, flying from airfields seized by the 1st Belarussian Front's tank armies and put into operation by the following airfield engineer and service battalions. The 193rd Fighter Division's 347th Fighter Regiment landed at Tempelhof airfield after its capture, despite ongoing fighting in the area and antiaircraft fire. German mortars fired at the first fighters to land, piloted by regimental commander Lieutenant Colonel P. B. Dankevich and his wingman, but were soon silenced and the regiment began to use Tempelhof for operations over Berlin. The same day, the 517th and 518th Fighter Regiments from the same division established operations from the recently captured Berlin airport at Schoenfeld.

Novikov set up two air control posts to direct air operations amidst the intense block-to-block fighting. The deputy commander of the 16th Air Army, General Aleksandr Senatorov, ran the primary CP in eastern Berlin, while General Boris Tokarev, the commander of the 6th Ground Attack Corps, ran a second in the northern part of the city. No Soviet air strikes could be launched without clearance and direction from these control posts. VVS officers and communications personnel set up rooftop observation posts to report the position of the front line and relay requests for airstrikes. Radio, lights, and flares were used to communicate with the aircraft, allowing pinpoint attacks on German strongpoints.

Luftflotte 6 commander Greim was abruptly ordered to report to the Fuhrerbunker in the midst of the battle. Greim flew to Berlin on April 25 with his fiancée, the famous German test pilot Hannah Reitsch, flying first in a Ju 188 and then an Fw 190, escorted by 12

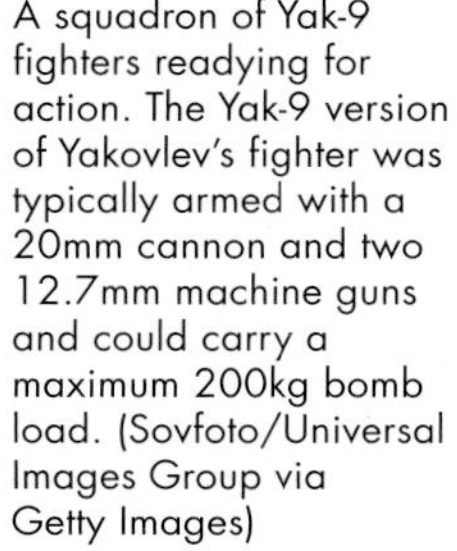

A squadron of Yak-9 fighters readying for action. The Yak-9 version of Yakovlev's fighter was typically armed with a 20mm cannon and two 12.7mm machine guns and could carry a maximum 200kg bomb load. (Sovfoto/Universal Images Group via Getty Images)

JG 26 Focke-Wulfs. Switching to a Fieseler Storch for the final run into the city, Greim was wounded in the foot by Soviet antiaircraft fire before landing at the improvised airstrip on the Tiergarten after Reitsch grabbed the controls. While Greim's wound was being dressed in the bunker, he discovered that Hitler had charged Goering with treason; Hitler had called Greim to his underground headquarters for promotion to field marshal and appointed him commander of the Luftwaffe. Three days later, Greim was ordered to arrest Himmler, who was trying to negotiate with the Western Allies, and Greim and Reitsch were able to fly out in an Arado Ar 96.

The final offensive into the city center was begun on April 26 by 464,000 Soviet troops, and the defenders appealed for supplies to be flown in. The Luftwaffe had made ambitious plans to provide 500 tons of supplies with 250 transport sorties, but only 115 miscellaneous transports could be gathered for the operation. With Tempelhof captured, German airmen were reduced to landing Ju 52s on a makeshift airstrip on the main east–west road through the city. The improvised runway was soon blocked by a crashed transport, after which the Germans turned to using Fw 190s and Bf 190s to drop supply containers, despite difficulties identifying the drop zones. In the end, about 200 supply sorties were flown at a cost of 30 aircraft shot down. KG 200 continued to attack the Oder bridges even as the Soviets closed in on the Reichstag. Mistels attacked the bridges on April 26, but of the seven dispatched, only two Fw 190s returned, with no confirmed hits. KG 200 was disbanded the next day, and like many Luftwaffe squadrons and air groups, its personnel were fed into nearby infantry units.

Over the city, thick smoke columns merged into a huge cloud up to 300 meters, limiting VVS airstrikes to only the most experienced crews. Over the next few days, the smoke and closeness of the fighting reduced calls for air support; the 16th Air Army flew 1,244 sorties on April 26, but only 809 and 93 respectively on the next two days. On the 29th, the Luftwaffe made a final effort over Berlin, with 346 sorties met by 1,603 from Redenko's air army. In 67 air engagements, the VVS claimed 46 victories for the loss of only two Soviet aircraft. On the 30th, Hitler committed suicide in the bunker. During the afternoon, troops of the 150th Rifle Division of Chuikov's 8th Guards Army fought their way to the roof of the Reichstag and raised the Red Banner over the devastated city. There was little air activity during the day over the city center, but 108 3rd Bomber Corps bombers attacked German positions southwest of Potsdam without Luftwaffe interference.

Battles against encircled enemy forces

The Red Army thrust to Berlin left the bulk of the 9th Army and 4th Panzer Army – what the Soviets referred to as the Frankfurt-Guben group – bypassed and encircled, but Hitler had demanded they launch attacks to relieve the capital. Konev and Zhukov relied heavily on the VVS to neutralize any threat to their flanks and rear areas, as only light ground elements had been detached to screen the pockets. On the night of April 21–22, a two-division force from the 4th Panzer Army pocket drove through the 48th Rifle Corps and overran the supply columns in the rear of the 2nd Polish Army near Cottbus. Krasovsky's 4th and 6th Bomber Corps silenced the German artillery and destroyed 12 tanks. The counterattack was held, with the 2nd Air Army ultimately flying 4,400 sorties and claiming 50 enemy tanks knocked out. Four days later, elements of the 9th Army massed to attack to the west to link up with the remnants of the 12th Army on the Elbe, and Krasvosky was forced to dedicate most 2nd Air Army bomber units to halt the attack. The 6th Guards Bomber Corps hit the crossings over the Dahm River with Pe-2s to prevent the linkup of the German armies, and the 4th Bomber Corps struck 9th Army columns. A raid by nine Il-10s of 108th Guards Ground Attack Regiment claimed 30 trucks destroyed. The next day, elements of both the 2nd and 16th Air Armies concentrated their firepower against 15km^2 of forested terrain and devastated the entire area.

VVS ground crews performing engine and weaponry maintenance. The VVS air army organization contained a capable and mobile ground support organization including airfield engineer and airfield support battalions. (Nik Cornish at www.Stavka.photos)

To finally eliminate the pocket, three armies from the 1st Belarussian Front and two from the 1st Ukrainian Front launched coordinated attacks from the north and south, supported by 1,000 aircraft of the 16th and 2nd Air Armies. Fighters intercepted Luftwaffe resupply flights, reconnaissance aircraft sought out German positions in the pocket, and free hunting Il-2s struck targets of opportunity. The Luftwaffe attempted to support the defenders, with 100 sorties on April 28, 74 on the 29th, and 76 on the 30th. The Germans sent 36 Me 262s into the battle, claiming to destroy 65 Soviet lorries and six Shturmoviks, but at least ten Me 262s were lost to Soviet fighters and ground fire between April 28 and May 1. The 2nd Air Army recorded that 23 percent of its sorties during the Berlin offensive – over 6,000 – were used against the pocket: 2,459 of these by Shturmoviks, 1,131 by bombers, 552 by night bombers, and 1,858 by fighters. VVS airmen delivered 4,850 tons of bombs and used 9,200 rockets. The pocket finally collapsed on May 1, the Soviets claiming 60,000 enemy killed and 120,000 taken prisoner.

The end in Berlin

During the night of April 30, a few Ju 52s flew over the city attempting to drop supplies. The final engagement between the Luftwaffe and 16th Air Army took place on May 1 as Yak-3s of the 233rd Fighter Regiment engaged four Fw 190s from JG 3, with Captain Viktor Yashin claiming two victories. The German garrison surrendered that night, and 480,000 troops entered Soviet prisoner of war camps. On May 1, the USSR's May Day holiday, 16 pilots of the 2nd Air Army flew over Berlin and parachuted Red Banners over the Reichstag to mark the victory. The next day, about 3,000 German troops attempting to break out to the west attacked Dalgow airfield, where the 265th Fighter Division was based. The fighters sortied and began to fire on the German attackers, while the 462nd and 609th Air Service Battalions and technical support personnel took up arms to defend the base perimeter. Late in the day, infantry, artillery, and tanks from the 125th Corps arrived to assist in the defense. Of the attackers, 379 were killed and 1,450 captured.

The VVS's three frontal air armies and the bombers of Golovanov's 18th Air Army flew a total of 91,000 sorties during the Berlin operation – 39,199 in support of Zhukov, 26,335 for Konev, and 25,490 for Rokossovsky. The Soviets claimed the destruction of 1,166 enemy aircraft for the loss of 917 to all causes. From April 16 to the end of the war, the US Eighth Air Force only reported downing 47 German aircraft, highlighting the concentration of Luftwaffe resources to defend Berlin in the last days of the conflict. Although undoubtedly inflated, the Soviet kill claims reflect VVS quantitative and qualitative air dominance; and although German airmen battled to the end over Berlin, the Luftwaffe was unable to make a significant impact on the ground war in its last days. Of 328 tanks lost by Konev's 1st Ukrainian Front from April 1 to May 9, only 27 were from German air attack.

Soviet air operations during the Berlin Operation, April 16–May 8, 1945

Date	16th Air Army sorties	18th Air Army sorties	2nd Air Army sorties	4th Air Army sorties	Total	Free hunt/airfield attack sorties	German aircraft claimed
April 16	5,342	768	3,546		9,656	239	205
April 17*	892	766	1,813		3,471	110	94
April 18	4,032	244	2,158		6,434	132	218
April 19	4,398		1,544		5,942	89	136
April 20	4,054		1,290	3,260	8,604	74	106
April 21*	539	548	845	849	2,781	28	41
April 22	3,864		1,221	3,020	8,105	128	39
April 23	1,586		814	2,113	4,513	104	50
April 24	2,345	111	1,998	2,500	6,954	202	75
April 25	2,979	563	2,573	3,034	9,149	203	66
April 26	1,244		2,328	2,641	6,213	159	20
April 27	809		1,583	2,176	4,568	134	16
April 28	93		133	272	498	10	
April 29	1,603		1,746	1,043	4,392	86	78
April 30	1,358		1,590	727	3,675	46	10
May 1	670		1,153	454	2,277	22	12
May 2	311			157	468		
May 3				910	910		
May 4				1,979	1,979		
May 5				85	85	8	
Totals	36,119	3,000	26,335	25,490	90,674	1,766	1,166

*adverse flying weather

The end in the East

South of the Carpathian Mountains, Soviet forces secured Hungary and – as Zhukov, Konev, and Rokossovsky massed for the Berlin offensive – attacked into Austria. Budapest was encircled in late December 1944, and, after intense urban combat and the defeat of an Axis relief attempt, fell in early January 1945. General Sergey Goryunov's 5th Air Army and General Vladimir Sudet's 17th Air Army battled Luftflotte 4 during the siege. Even with the loss of Budapest, the small Hungarian oilfields played an outsized role in Hitler's strategic calculations, and he sent his last strategic reserve – the still potent 6th SS Panzer Army – to launch a new offensive towards the Hungarian capital in March. The Soviets were forced into difficult defensive combat, aided by strikes by the Shturmoviks of Sudent's 17th Air Army against the German armor struggling forward in the deep snow. As the panzer attack ground to a halt, the Soviets unleashed a massive offensive on its northern flank and the Red Army reached Vienna's city center on April 8. Sudet's airmen had flown 24,100 sorties and Goryunov's 16,568. The cost for the campaign was 614 Soviet aircraft.

With the fall of Berlin, the remaining German forces were divided into northern and southern pockets. General Dessloch commanded the remnants of Luftflotte 4 in Bavaria, and Fiebig controlled what Luftwaffe assets remained north of Berlin. On May 8, Captain Erich Hartmann spotted and shot down a Yak while on a final reconnaissance flight for his 352nd and final kill. Hostilities in the European theater ceased at midnight May 8/9, and the last air combat of the war in Europe probably took place during the afternoon of the

The Luftwaffe fought to the end. The wreck of an Fw 190 after the fall of Berlin, with the Reichstag visible in the distance. (Mondadori Portfolio via Getty Images)

9th when Captain Vasiliy Pshenichikov, flying an Aircobra of the 100th Guards Fighter Regiment, intercepted and shot down an Fw 189 reconnaissance aircraft inspecting Soviet positions in Prague.

Greim was captured by American troops in Bavaria, and the last officer promoted to field marshal rank committed suicide soon after, probably with cyanide given to him by Hitler in the Fuhrerbunker. General Fiebig was captured by the British, handed over to Yugoslavia, and executed for war crimes in 1947. Rudel, the Stuka ace, remained an unrepentant admirer of Hitler and emigrated to Argentina, while Eric Hartmann endured ten years of captivity in the USSR, and after his release commanded the first all-jet unit in West Germany's reborn Luftwaffe. Soviet air force leaders faced a new wave of purges after the war. Novikov was brutally interrogated by the NKVD (secret police) and imprisoned, and after his release upon Stalin's death in 1953 did not return to active service. Marshal S. A. Khudyaov, who served as VVS Chief of Staff and deputy commander during the war, was executed in 1950. Others fared better, Vershinin being promoted to marshal in 1946 and becoming VVS commander-in-chief from 1946–49 and later from 1957–69. Long-Range Aviation leader Golovanov remained as head of the bomber force until, possibly due to his close relationship with Stalin, he left the service after the dictator's death in 1953.

AFTERMATH AND ANALYSIS

The fronts of the Red Army and their supporting VVS air armies had driven from Warsaw to Berlin in five months, while other Soviet ground and air forces south of the Carpathian Mountains secured Hungary and Austria. As the Nazi regime surrendered, the forces of the USSR and Western Allies met on the Elbe, and Patton's and Konev's forces in Czechoslovakia. Losses to the Luftwaffe are difficult to calculate, as the force was utterly destroyed by the end of the war, with its stockpiles of aircraft destroyed or seized by the Allies for technical exploitation. The cost to the VVS had been 3,750 aircraft from January to May 1945 – a monthly loss rate similar to those of 1943 and 1944. VVS losses were heaviest in the aircraft that were most heavily dedicated to ground attack roles – the Il-2M in particular, but also the Pe-2 light bomber and the Yak-9, often used for bombing and strafing attacks in 1945.

Soviet pilots scrambling for their Lavochkin fighters. By 1945, the VVS was able to field much better prepared pilots. In contrast, the Luftwaffe's training program had to be constantly shortened to replace their losses and the majority of its pilots in 1945 entered combat with extremely limited preparation. (Courtesy of the Central Museum of the Armed Forces, Moscow via www.Stavka.photos)

Soviet bomber and ground attack aircraft losses in 1945								
	Pe-2	Tu-2	PS-84/Li-2	Il-4	A-20	B-25	Il-2M	Total
Number lost	358	2	19	54	142	16	1,691	2,282

Soviet fighter losses in 1945								
	Yak-1	Yak-3	Yak-7	Yak-9	La-5	La-7	Kobra	Total
Number lost	79	150	12	448	233	79	190	1,191

Luftwaffe performance

The Luftwaffe had fought to the end with ingenuity and tenacity, and played a significant role in delaying the Soviet offensive against Berlin. The 1944 hopes that new technology weapons such as the V-1 and V-2, or massed surprise attacks like the *Bodenplatte* New Year's Day raid, would give a decisive advantage had proven bankrupt. Luftwaffe leaders continued to pursue all possible means to improve effectiveness, using obsolete biplanes for night operations, launching Mistel composite bombers against rail bridges, and mounting infantry Panzerschreck bazookas on fighter bombers. After the Soviet offensive to the Oder in January, the Luftwaffe on the Eastern Front received priority for pilots and aircraft and operated as intensely as the limited fuel supplies allowed. While Me 262s and other new technology weapons were employed against the Western Allies, the pilots of the Eastern Front, flying a mixed force of Fw 190s along with numbers of Stukas and obsolete biplanes, had the most impact on the course of events in 1945. Weather, long Soviet lines of communications, and Stalin's strategic decisions gave the Luftwaffe an opportunity to seize air superiority in early February. Able to operate from concrete airfields in the Reich, German airmen managed to briefly wrest control of the air from the VVS and halt Zhukov on the Oder, playing a significant role in the Soviet decision to delay the final offensive on Berlin – a decision that arguably extended the war by another three months.

By late February, the VVS numerical and qualitative superiority reasserted itself, and the Luftwaffe could only struggle – vastly outnumbered – to stave off the inevitable. Squadrons nevertheless flew until out of fuel or until their bases were overrun. Rudel, flying again despite the amputation of his leg, led the three remaining Ju 87s and four Fw 190s of SG 3 on a last attack run against Soviet tanks in Czechoslovakia before setting down at a US-held airfield, with the pilots purposely landing hard to collapse the landing gear. Numerous other Luftwaffe pilots loaded as many base personnel as possible behind their cockpits and took off as Soviet troops approached their airfields to surrender to the Western Allies.

The VVS

The Soviet Air Force that defeated its outnumbered opponents in 1945 was a powerful weapon, well-honed to support the massive Red Army offensives that smashed German defenses in Poland, East Prussia, and Berlin. VVS leadership, logistics, and command and control, along with aircraft, pilot, and aircrew quality, had matured, giving the force a qualitative as well as quantitative edge over its hard-pressed Luftwaffe opponents. VVS operations during 1945 demonstrated an excellent capability to mass and control airpower, with Novikov and his staff able to control three air armies and Baltic Fleet aviation over Konigsberg and four air armies during the Berlin campaign. VVS commanders proved adept at flexibly using their air assets. Once the tank armies had broken through the enemy front, Soviet strike aircraft provided close support to the advancing armor, just as the USAAF and RAF tactical air forces supported Montgomery's and Patton's dash across France. During the Berlin operation, the VVS demonstrated its ability to screen, neutralize, and destroy the encircled German 12th and 9th Army pockets while securing air superiority over the city and providing precision strikes for the attacking Red Army ground forces.

The USSR rigorously prioritized the mass production of military material, in particular tanks and aircraft, during the Great Patriotic War. By the end of the conflict the Soviets had produced 114,719 combat aircraft and had received 13,904 fighters, 3,653 bombers, and 1,011 other aircraft from the Western Allies. (Universal History Archive via Getty Images)

Soviet air power was fully integrated with ground force schemes of maneuver and served as an extension of the massive artillery bombardments that opened all major Red Army attacks. Postwar analysis by Soviet military theorists calculated that Soviet aviation forces flew roughly four million combat sorties during the war, with the air armies of frontal aviation and the long-range bomber force flying 3,124,000 of those. Soviet analysts considered 46.5 percent of these were in direct support of ground operations, 35 percent air superiority missions, 11 percent reconnaissance, and 5.4 percent strategic strikes. In reality, almost all fighter, ground attack, and bomber sorties were used to conduct or escort close air support to the ground forces. The Soviet conception of air superiority involved its fighter forces closely escorting bomber and ground attack aircraft, with a much lower percentage dedicated to attacking enemy airfields or flying free hunt patrols to seek out enemy aircraft. The Pe-2 and Tu-2 bombers of the frontal air armies and the long-range bombers of the 18th Air Army delivered the vast majority of their strikes against targets just to the rear of the enemy front line or against lines of communication, reserves, or headquarters within a few miles of the front.

The Soviet doctrinal approach to air operations provided powerful support for the ground forces but used little of its power to strike deeper behind the enemy front line. Long-Range Aviation was a force almost completely composed of twin-engine medium bombers and predominantly targeted enemy forces near the front line and railway yards that could be used to move up reinforcements. In recognition of this reality, the force lost its independent status in December 1944 and was re-formed as the 18th Air Army and placed under VVS command. With the notable exception of the April 7 daylight attack on Konigsberg, its raids were confined to nighttime hours and were only able to attack area targets. Soviet analyses of the 18th Air Army operations during 1945 indicate 8,398 sorties bombing in support of the ground forces, 5,066 against rail targets near the front, 1,399 against ports, and only 106 against enemy airfields.

The VVS also gave little emphasis to deep interdiction strikes, raids against enemy airfields, or offensive fighter sweeps. The VVS inflicted heavy losses on the Luftwaffe in the air, especially when guided by its network of radars and radio relay centers, but typically held its fighters close to the front to cover preparations for an offensive, or to escort aircraft on reconnaissance, ground attack, or bombing missions. Even during the Berlin operation, the three engaged frontal air armies only dedicated 2 percent of their sorties to free hunt patrols or attacks on enemy airfields. In contrast, Western air doctrine, exemplified by the Luftwaffe's surprise attacks on Soviet airfields in the very first hours of Operation *Barbarossa* in 1941, called for the elimination of an enemy air force, preferably on the ground, to secure theater-wide air superiority and then to exploit it with operations in support of ground forces. In 1944, the Western Allies prepared for D-Day with offensive air operations to weaken the Luftwaffe and systematic deep interdiction efforts to isolate the Normandy battlefield. As the VVS put much less emphasis on such operations, the heavily outnumbered Luftwaffe managed to remain a force in being that could still meet and fight the Soviets on relatively even terms during the last years of the war in select zones of operation.

As with all nations' air forces during World War II, VVS operations were hindered by poor weather conditions, especially during the winter months of 1945. The shift of the start of the January offensive to a period of front-wide poor weather prevented the five air armies supporting the assault across the Vistula and into East Prussia from executing their planned sorties for several days. Only the return of good flying weather on January 16 allowed the Soviets to fly in large numbers, and to the north, the airmen of the 4th and 1st Air Armies to play a critical role in supporting breakthroughs by Rokossovsky's and Chernyakovsky's forces. The early February thaw crippled VVS operations over the Oder River as it struggled to operate from forward airstrips now turned to mud. Even during the Berlin operation, the combination of morning fog and the smoke raised by the huge Soviet preliminary bombardments forced the supporting air armies to abort many of the sorties planned for the early hours of the attack.

Cold war legacy

May 1945 saw the VVS at the peak of its power, and its operations during the war were closely studied by Soviet military scientists and planners throughout the Cold War. Nevertheless, even as the victors gathered at Potsdam, Stalin and his high command realized that Soviet military aviation urgently required modernization. VVS aircraft lacked the range and payload of many of their Western counterparts, and the USSR's aviation industry was not yet capable of building significant numbers of four-engine bombers or jet aircraft. The USAAF soon inaugurated a new chapter in strategic air warfare with the delivery of atomic weapons by the long-range B-29 bomber. Before his arrest, Novikov drafted a letter to Stalin outlining the VVS's need to develop modern capabilities, including long-range bombers, radar-equipped night fighters, and jet propulsion.

The means to jump-start modernization were directly at hand, as Soviet troops had overrun and captured the bulk of the German weapons research and production infrastructure, moved eastward to attempt to avoid Allied strategic bombing raids. Germany was the world-leader in jet engines and guided missile development, and the Soviets were able to seize numerous facilities such as the Junkers engine factory at Bernburg, complete with the Me 262's Jumo 004 turbojet engines and prototypes for improved designs, and the Walter factory in Prague with the newest Me 262 interceptors. Just as valuable were the engineers and scientists from the programs located in the Soviet occupation zone and transported to the USSR in 1946 to continue their work in special closed facilities. Three US B-29 bombers had made emergency landings in the Soviet Far East before the USSR entered the war against Japan, and Andrey Tupolev was tasked to lead an effort to produce a Soviet version. The resulting Tu-4 was a close analog of the US bomber, but with Soviet engines and defensive machine guns replaced with 23mm cannon. Tu-4s flew with first-generation Yak-15 and MiG-9 jet fighters over the 1947 May Day parade in Moscow, alarming Western observers. In 1949, the Soviet Union tested an atomic weapon, and thermonuclear weapons would follow. By the next year, the VVS's superb jet fighter, the MiG-15, would duel with US Air Force F-86 Sabers over the Yalu River, most flown by Chinese or Korean communist pilots but some by covertly posted Soviet veterans of the Great Patriotic War.

Soviet ground crew loading a 2-ton FAB-2000 high explosive bomb on one of the few Pe-8s available to its long-range bomber force. Despite its name, LRA had only a handful of Pe-8s and consisted almost entirely of Il-4, B-25 Mitchell, and A-20 Boston/Havoc bombers. (Courtesy of the Central Museum of the Armed Forces, Moscow via www.Stavka.photos)

By the late 1950s, a new Luftwaffe, led by a number of veterans of World War II, was being formed and would play a major role in NATO airpower during the Cold War. Other Luftwaffe veterans, including the airlift expert Morzik, were writing accounts of aerial combat with the Soviets for the US military to serve as guides for US planners. On the other side of the Iron Curtain, the legacy of 1945 also remained, with jet fighters and fighter bombers of the 16th Air Army now stationed in the Democratic Republic of Germany – the Soviet zone – and planning to execute a new air offensive should the Warsaw Pact forces be called to attack towards the Rhine. For decades, new generations of aircraft, still marked with the German cross and the red star, stood ready for a potential new struggle, based on the lessons of 1945 aerial combat, but with the new MiG, Sukoy, and Tupolev jets now carrying nuclear weapons.

FURTHER READING

Information on air operations on the Eastern Front in 1945 is limited and scattered among a variety of works. Glantz and House's *When Titans Clashed* covers the entire war in the East but includes an excellent overview of 1945 operations, and the last year of the war is covered in detail in the Erickson, Ziemke, and Beevor books below, but these works overwhelmingly focus on ground operations. Duffy's *Red Storm on the Reich* provides an in-depth survey of Red Army operations against Germany in 1945 with a useful examination of German and Soviet operational art, but lacks an in-depth discussion of the final offensive against Berlin. Zaloga's Osprey campaign volume covers operations both on the Eastern and Western Fronts in April and May, with Antill's providing more detail on the battle for Berlin itself. Both of the studies by the Soviet General Staff cited below give good insight into VVS planning to support offensives in 1945, although the bulk of these works cover ground operations.

For air operations, Hooton's *War over the Steppes* gives an excellent overview, with some coverage of 1945, as does von Hardesty's overview of the Soviet air effort, *Red Pheonix*. Kozhevnikov's *The Command and Staff of the Soviet Army Air Force in the Great Patriotic War* and *The Soviet Air Force in World War II*, translated by Wagner, are Cold War-era books but do give some insight into Soviet command operations as well as useful statistics on the VVS. For air operations during the last year of the war, Price's *The Last Year of the Luftwaffe: May 1944 to May 1945*, is useful, although it devotes most of its attention to German new technology weapons and operations in the West. Bergstrom's *Bagration to Berlin* includes excellent detail on the clash between Soviet and German airmen in the East, with the last several chapters covering operations in 1945.

The campaign

Antill, Peter, *Berlin 1945: The End of the Thousand Year Reich*, Osprey (2005).

Beevor, Antony, *The Fall of Berlin 1945*, Viking, New York (2002).

Duffy, Christopher, *Red Storm on the Reich: the Soviet March on Germany, 1945*, Castle Books (1990).

Erickson, John, *The Road to Berlin: Continuing the History of Stalin's War with Germany*, Westview Press, Boulder, Colorado (1983).

Glantz, David M. & House, Jonathan M., *When Titans Clashed: How the Red Army Stopped Hitler*, revised edition, University of Kansas Press, Lawrence (2015).

Soviet General Staff, *The Berlin Operation 1945*, edited and translated by Richard W. Harrison, Helion & Company, published in cooperation with the Association of the United States Army (2016).

Soviet General Staff, *Prelude to Berlin: The Red Army's Offensive Operations in Poland and Eastern Germany, 1945*, edited and translated by Richard W. Harrison, Helion & Company, published in cooperation with the Association of the United States Army (2016).

Zaloga, Steven, *Downfall 1945: The Fall of Hitler's Third Reich*, Osprey (2016).

Ziemke, Earl F., *Stalingrad to Berlin: The German Defeat in the East*, Office of the Chief of Military History, United States Army (1968).

The Luftwaffe and VVS

Bergstrom, Christer, *Bagration to Berlin, the Final Air Battles in the East, 1944–1945*, Ian Allen Publishing, Hersham, Surrey (2008).

Forsyth, Robert, *Luftwaffe Mistel Composite Bomber Units*, Osprey (2015).

Hardesty, Von & Grindberg, Ilya, *Red Pheonix Rising: The Soviet Air Force in World War II*, University of Kansas Press, Lawrence (2012).

Hooton, E. R., *War Over the Steppes: The Air Campaigns on the Eastern Front 1941–45*, Osprey Publishing (2016).

Khazanov, Dmitry & Medved, Aleksander, *La-5/7 vs Fw 190; Eastern Front 1942–45*, Osprey Publishing (2011).

Kozhevnikov, M. N., *The Command and Staff of the Soviet Army Air Force in the Great Patriotic War: A Soviet View*, University Press of the Pacific, Honolulu, Hawaii (2005, reprint of 1977 edition).

Mellinger, George, *LaGG & Lavochkin Aces of World War 2*, Osprey Publishing (2003).

Mellinger, George, *Soviet Lend-Lease Fighter Aces of World War 2*, Osprey Publishing (2006).

Muller, Dr Richard R., "Losing Air Superiority: A Case Study from the Second World War" in *Air & Space Power Journal*, Vol. 14, Issue 4, Winter (2003), pp.55–66.

Price, Alfred, *The Last Year of the Luftwaffe: May 1944 to May 1945*, Motorbooks Inc., Osceola, WI (1991).

Price, Alfred, *The Luftwaffe Data Book*, Greenhill Books, London (1977).

Rudel, Hans-Ulrich, *Stuka Pilot*, New Edition, Black House Publishing, London (2012).

Wagner, Ray (ed.), *The Soviet Air Force in World War II: The Official History, Originally Published by the Ministry of Defense of the USSR*, Doubleday & Company (1973).

Weal, John, *Focke-Wulf Fw 190 Aces of the Russian Front*, Osprey Publishing (1995).

Weal, John, *Luftwaffe Schlachtgruppen*, Osprey Publishing (2003).

Whiting, Kenneth R., "Soviet Air–Ground Coordination, 1941–1945" in Benjamin Franklin Cooling (ed.), *Case Studies in the Development of Close Air Support,* Special Studies, Office of Air Force History, United States Air Force, 1990.